POF ETITION

IINDS

Your World...Your Future...YOUR WORDS

From London Vol I
Edited by Lynsey Hawkins

 Young**Writers**

First published in Great Britain in 2005 by:
Young Writers
Remus House
Coltsfoot Drive
Peterborough
PE2 9JX
Telephone: 01733 890066
Website: www.youngwriters.co.uk

SB ISBN 1 84460 708 9

Foreword

This year, the Young Writers' 'Great Minds' competition proudly presents a showcase of the best poetic talent selected from over 40,000 up-and-coming writers nationwide.

Young Writers was established in 1991 to promote the reading and writing of poetry within schools and to the youth of today. Our books nurture and inspire confidence in the ability of young writers and provide a snapshot of poems written in schools and at home by budding poets of the future.

The thought, effort, imagination and hard work put into each poem impressed us all and the task of selecting poems was a difficult but nevertheless enjoyable experience.

We hope you are as pleased as we are with the final selection and that you and your family continue to be entertained with *Great Minds From London Vol I* for many years to come.

Contents

Bishop Challoner Catholic Collegiate School

Hampstead School

Serena Manteghi (16)	49
Leanne Chorekdjian (14)	50
Scarlet Fallon-O'Sullivan (13)	51
Gemma Ross (13)	52
Ander Fraser (16)	53
Shireen Qureshi (16)	54
Alex Nqai (13)	55
Kitty Jenkins (16)	56
Lilybeth King (13)	57
Maxine Ellah (14)	58
Terri Morris (16)	59
Leah Devlin (14)	60
Nicholas Courtman (13)	60
Anna Robin (16)	61
Fjerza Bekteshi (13)	61
Lyria Eastley (16)	62
Marcelino Rey (16)	63
Oscar McLaughlin (13)	64
Iyanu Taiwo (16)	65
Quaam Animashaun (16)	66
Thomas Petrie (14)	66
Lauren Watters (16)	67
Tiffany Dowden (13)	67
Nora Nilsen (16)	68
Alexander Wainstok (13)	69
Kirsty O'Neill (16)	70
Jennifer Gildea (13)	71
Julian Marton (13)	72
James Woods-Segura (13)	73

Holloway School

Tunde Yusuff (11)	73
Jamal Gayle (15)	74
Oliver Beccles (15)	75
Lakaia Chapman (12)	75
Daniel Mantey (14)	76
Ben Kinsella (13)	76
Conor Jones (12)	77
Dagmawit Amdemichael (13)	77

Ryan Wenzel (13)   78
Chloe Hester (12)   78

Islamia Girls' School
Fahima Khan (11)   79
Esma Al-Sibai (11)   79
Nashwa Ali (11)   80
Zainab Arshad (11)   80
Amina Hassan (11)   81
Zeynep Tahir (11)   81
Ameena Majeed (11)   81
Amna Sabih (11)   82
Sana Ali (11)   82
Mariam Haidour (11)   83
Hafsah Aaqab (11)   83
Zahra Faiz (11)   83
Ruba Ramadan (11)   84
Bayan Cevahir (11)   85

James Allen's Girls' School
Sarah Wedmore (15)   85
Alison Eson (13)   86
Sophie Renner (15)   87
Olivia Cerio (15)   88
Liz Burgess (15)   89
Jess Austin (14)   90
Alex Wilson (11)   91
Cecily Cole (15)   92
Katie George (11)   93
Kei Lawford (15)   94
Helen Oxenham (16)   95

La Sainte Union School
Annabelle Appiah-Dankwah (15)   95
Katherine Wise (13)   96
Valentina Okolo (11)   97
Liza Turkova (13)   98
Kasia Giddings (12)   98
Kemi Odunlami (14)   99
Mary-Grace Sturley (15)   99

Notre Dame RC Girls' School

North Bridge House School

Ursuline High School

Kathleen Cabigas (12)	178
Paige Rippon (12)	179
Aamina Qazi (12)	180
Fisayo Fadahunsi (11)	181
Anne Felice Soria	181
Alia-Michelle Supron (13)	182
Stephanie Campbell (14)	182
Amy Luck (12)	183
Jade Nartey	184
Rosalyn Duffy (13)	184
Nathalie Moorghen (13)	185
Sophia Kyriacou (13)	185
Toya Islam-Sanchez	186
Philippa Mann (12)	186
Rebecca McGrath (12)	187
Courtney Vincent (13)	188
Ariana Remuiñan (13)	189
Arti Vaghela (11)	190
Niamh Proctor (11)	191
Elvira Pandolfi (13)	192
Tania Nadarajah	193
Caroline Draper (13)	194
Elizabeth Lau (11)	194
Helen Folkard-Baker (12)	195
Rebecca Heath (13)	196
Zubeida Osman (12)	197
Anne Attipoe	198
Kayeesha Gomes (12)	198
Catherine Furlong (12)	199
Nancy Fagan (12)	200
Hannah Best (13)	201
Aimee Cunningham (12)	201
Lucy Rawlings (12)	202
Dannielle Leonard (12)	202
Charlotte Napoleon-Kuofie (12)	203
Helen Tanner (12)	204
Lucy McDonald (13)	204
Katie Kemp (11)	205
Natasha D'souza (12)	205
Massah Tucker (12)	206

The Poems

Things Change

In the beginning of time,
No war, no crime,
No abuse, no drugs,
No human thugs –
Things change . . .

As I'm sitting in bed,
Fears running through my head,
'Will I be here tomorrow?'
'Will terrorists fill my soul with sorrow?'
'Will I see my mum? Any unborn son?'
'Can I contemplate ever having fun?'
When I'm so scared my emotions flared,
Sitting with fears, my insides drowned with tears,
Things have changed . . .

At this moment in time,
There's war, there's crime,
There's abuse, there's drugs,
There's human thugs,
Can things change? . . .

Can we tell the people that are so hurt,
We don't agree with Tony's blood-red shirt?
That we want things to change . . .

To go back to the beginning when the world wasn't so deranged.

I want to be able to say . . .

At this moment in time,
No war, no crime,
No abuse, no drugs,
No human thugs -

But that would be a lie,
And we've all had enough of those . . .

Rosa Jesse (14)

Bad Day At School

The ball's gone through the windowpane
Susie and Joe are kissing again.

Maths today was such a drag,
My homework got torn in my bag.

Running down the corridor,
Detentions, punishments, trouble galore!

To the flowers janitor tends
Teacher has gone round the bend.

School lunch today was curried mush,
Form tutors are all in a rush.

Reading, 'riting, 'rithmetic,
Small bits of paper we flick.

There's a boy balancing knives called Kurt,
Oooooooooh man, that's gotta hurt!

Bell rings and falls off the wall,
Confiscation of the ball.

Dirty shoes, scruffy shirt,
Annoying new lad called Albert.

Headmaster comes to break it up,
Bang him on the head with a plastic cup!

I gave in my homework late,
Head comes to decide my fate.

'What excuse is it, then?'
'The book got eaten by a hen!'

I get home and slam the door,
Plonk my bag down on the floor.

Spent the day breaking many a rule,
What a terrible day at school!

Robbie Haylett (11)
Alleyns School

The Flood

Sudden thunder hurls its broken sword,
Splitting night in blinding rain,
Again the storm is from the Lord:
Doling out the heathen pain.

His eyes fizz brilliance to the gloom,
Booming voice of retribution,
Elocution of heavenly doom,
Womb of distant revolution.

Hurls the torrents down in rage,
Age of power now unfurls,
Curls the lightning fingers, wage
Sage war with bolts of pearls.

But the Lord is merciful and knows
That Noah floats as the current flows.

Rocco Sulkin (17)
Alleyns School

My Recipe For Love . . .

First start with two hearts.
Mix a bowl of love and share evenly into each heart.
Add a teaspoon of hope and a dash of forgiveness to the love.
The love should now be a sweet, melt in the mouth texture.
Leave to set solid and strong; this will make sure the love
does not seep out and stays in the heart.
Bake in the oven for a few minutes until golden.
Take out and sprinkle with icing sugar to sweeten.
Serve with two faithful bodies and a sprig of luck.

Enjoy and, if prepared properly, this dish will last for eternity.

Gemma Hitchens (12)
Alleyns School

Word – Painting

I'm beginning again.
My life is a blank sheet of paper,
Unlike the last one
(Torn, dog-eared, scribbles).
I want to paint myself
Some time, maybe a little red
For love, perhaps possibly
Blue (calm) but above all
I want to paint myself
Some time.
Something aesthetically pleasing,
I Hope.

If you mess it up
One more time with that damned black pen,
I think I'm going to run out of paper.
And then what would I do
With all this
Paint?

Hannah Tottenham (15)
Alleyns School

Who Knows?

I sleep in a bomb shelter of plant pots,
Which is not made of saucepans or sausages,
My bed is made of dead butterflies but not moths,
I paint pictures in my head with lots of made up colours
But never on paper,
I hate poems,
I don't know whose this is so it's mine.

Peter Morton (11)
Alleyns School

An Evening On The Beach

Sunset has fallen
All over the land
Treasures lay hidden
Underneath the golden sand.

I sit there watching,
The tide comes in
Slowly, and slowly
There's peace within.

I see a seagull
Flying so freely
Its gleaming eyes
Beam down upon me.

I look across at the sun
With its shining light,
Oh what a beautiful
Beautiful night.

The breeze blows gently,
Not too heavily
As the sun sets lower
Gracefully and steadily.

The sun has gone down
And darkness takes over the sea
But I still sit there
Hugging my knees.

It's time to go
But I don't want to leave
This beach is mine
It belongs to me!

Angelfaith Locken (11)
Alleyns School

Food, Glorious Food

An apple, a pear, a banana
Spaghetti and potatoes too
You might love them too much
But they'll always be good for you.

Sausages, bacon and beans
The perfect feast for me
A breakfast prepared for loving
If you want, you can have it with tea.

What do you want? Fish and chips
With some garlic bread for two
You go to a restaurant, have this
Make sure you don't eat any goo.

Muffins, éclairs and pastries
Dairy Milk, Twix and KitKat
Ice cream, cakes and choccie mouse
Eat these but don't get fat.

Food, glorious food
It makes life worth living
Fruit, veg and sweets
Lots and lots of treats.

I love eating, who doesn't?
All foods are delicious
Supermarkets providing it all
Food is scrummylicious.

Alex Rowe (11)
Alleyns School

Simple, But Complex

When I am sleepy, life's
Simplicity wakes me up.
Those dull, simple days.

Then I think about life,
The world of humans,
The complex atoms.

She gives me power,
The bird of nature,
How simple is she?

Simplicity in herself,
But a cross stitch of
Complicated patterns.

All I think about all day is
What complex life gives me:
Happiness.

So I may drift
Through the simple stars
Above.

Mary Hamilton (11)
Alleyns School

The Perfect Garden

A gentle robin redbreast hopping on the fence,
Flowers in full bloom, in the middle of the hedge.
Large, proud fruit trees, sturdy and strong,
Bright green grass, getting far too long!
Tall, lush plants growing straight up,
In a crack in the patio, a tiny buttercup.
Carrots, parsnips, lettuce in the vegetable patch,
Children using the garden, on the lawn playing catch.

Jessica Webster (12)
Alleyns School

Old

All we can do is watch and wait
Until the paltry span of days that we call life
Runs out.
Then nothing is left to us but to walk upon
The path of our youth
Alone,
Life but a memory,
To see, to hear, to touch,
Theirs is the time that was ours,
A bright place of sounds and colours
Fades to a silent world of spirits
And so it goes on,
As they walk upon the paths we knew,
We go on,
An age of weariness and pain,
Unending, only by death.

Anna Tobenhouse (13)
Alleyns School

Autumn

I sit forever watching the autumn trees
As they transform into a magical array of different colours:
From greens and yellows to oranges, reds and browns
I see the leaves float gently downwards,
Into an orchestra of colours on the covered ground
The scene is beautiful; the colours merge in together
Like they are on a palette, ready for an artist to paint.

I notice the days begin to shorten as winter draws nearer
The trees become empty of their warm and sheltering leaves
The sight of sun is rare now,
Now it is for certain that summer has left us
Autumn is here.

Elizabeth Kinch (11)
Alleyns School

The Forcefulness

The flowing nib
That creates the magic
That creates the rise, fall, rise
Of someone's mind.

The pausing pen
That stops, thinks, decides
On someone's life or death
Just by one word.

The simple letters,
Capturing people's thoughts,
Creating good and evil
Thrive and decay.

The collection of words
Making up the beast, the angel,
The life, or cutting it short.
The story.

Luke Bell (12)
Alleyns School

An Old Bicycle

His skin flaky, joints creaky
Dirt smeared all over
Joints creaking every step he took
His body greasy and oily.

But even if I'm down he never fails to cheer me up
Never failing to amuse me
Always helping me get to places I want to go
If I had the choice I would never get a new bike.

Benedict Stephens Hemingway (11)
Alleyns School

A New Day

It's a new day today,
Tomorrow will be too,
Every day is a new day,
For me and you,
School will be different,
Maybe dinner too,
Every day is a new day,
For me and you,
Tomorrow may be horrid,
The day after that too,
Every day is a new day,
For me and you,
Yesterday was a fun day,
The day before that too,
Every day is a new day,
For me and you.

Ella Ackland (11)
Alleyns School

The Snake

Lazily draped across a branch of a tree
Silently waiting for its prey
Tongue flicking in and out licking its lips
Bored with nothing happening,
England fans at a football match,
Slithers easily across the branch like a tightrope walker in a circus
Drops to the ground, a skydiver out of a plane
Rears up about to strike
Hisses angrily he misses the prey
Strikes again like a bullet out of a gun
Stuffs the prey into its mouth like children without
Any table manners,
Lays back and relaxes after a well-earned meal
Then disappears back into the crowd of whispering trees.

Jamie Miller (11)
Alleyns School

Fog

It crawls through the city
Misty and dull
A grey without ghost.

It covers the land
With its dark cloak
A black creeping ghost.

It moves along the road
Swallowing up the houses
An evil, deadly ghost.

It races around the harbour
Knocking out the light
A colourless ghost.

It glides through towns
Searching for its lost soul
A dark, angry fog.

Ben Browett (11)
Alleyns School

Flower

The flower standing by itself
Graceful in every way.

As the pink veil falls
Over its smiling face
And the wind blows at its dainty face

It spreads the seeds of hope and joy
The flower is no longer alone.

She has friends.

Holly Ewart (11)
Alleyns School

The Candy Sheep

There, standing in front of me
A white, fluffy sheep
It is clean, like white candyfloss
Its gummy eyes staring at me unblinkingly.

It wandered aimlessly
Over to a patch of grass
And lay down, looking contented
The fluff on its body, swaying with the wind.

It looked now
Like it was unaware
Of me standing there
It got up, fell over and looked at me bluntly.

The white candyfloss has gone now
Only the stick is left, lying on the ground
The spirit of the sheep has gone now
Only the sheep is left, lying on the ground.

Camilla Craker-Horton (11)
Alleyns School

Thundercloud

A stormy black cloud looms overhead,
Its menacing flashes rolling out from it,
Booming as if it were a drum.

It hurls ice, as if it were angry,
Gigantic above me,
Like a giant coming towards me.

Louis Nicholson (11)
Alleyns School

Football

The whistle blows
And everyone goes
For the black and white ball,
The black and white ball.

They have a kick,
They're right in the thick
For the black and white ball
The black and white ball.

The man slides in,
The cardinal sin
For the black and white ball
The black and white ball.

The black and white ball,
In the goal it pops,
The black and white ball,
Then everything stops.

Sam Allen (12)
Alleyns School

Flowers

Flowers are so quiet,
That you never would have thought,
That when the clock strikes midnight,
They talk, and talk, and talk.

If you look at petals,
They look like tiny tears
But if you look more closely,
They're really tiny ears.

And as flowers can see and hear,
And talk so much as well,
You never would have thought,
That they have no sense of smell!

Scarlett Marshall (11)
Alleyns School

Recipe For A Perfect Day

Take one clear day making sure the sky is fresh and clean.
Add a sprinkling of soft clouds at the edges.
Next take a warm glowing sun checking that the temperature
Isn't too hot.
Stir in a gentle breeze enough to fill the sails of a yacht.
Mix in three fun-filled good friends.
Fold in a bowl of the softest, whitest sand and a jug of turquoise
Crystal sea.
Carefully pour in a dozen dolphins.
Stir slowly until mixed well and set aside for two hours.
Then take a piece of India.
Stir in a bag full of vibrant colours adding a pinch of exotic flavours
To taste.
Place in the centre one beautifully wrinkled elephant and carefully
Bring the mixture together.
Serve on a large never-ending plate and garnish with a winning
Lottery ticket.

Alice Hoskins (12)
Alleyns School

Old Rock Candy

He looked at me; rolling along the shelf,
Spreading cold-heartedness.

He was faded, old, breaking, decayed,
He looked at me, cold eyed.

Crack - broken
I found kindness, softness inside.

> Only on the deathbed does the person
> Within reveal its true identity.

Shadi Brazell (11)
Alleyns School

The Freshinoscent Fledgling

(In the style of E E Cummings)

the FrEshinoscent
fledglinG Sits in hIs Nest
In his trEequietly ObseRv
(iNg The New WoRLd) He seeS the world
Through unused
EyeS And sees it in
(AnoTher way)
He seeS the Flowers
and BirdS Darting through
the hedge. He feEls their joy
and senSes their mirth even though
He does not understan-d why, He marvels
At the sound of his voiCeBut Does Not Know
Why. Then a cat slinks up to the tRee,
And the fledglinG Looks Down Happily
And meets the Cat's Malicious
STare With merry Eyes, EveN when the
Cat ClimbS Along The
branch The fledgling
does not know.
eveN whEn
HiS mother
SCREECHES
He does
Not know
Then IT is too
Late And The
FledgLinG KNOWS.

Guy Carr (11)
Alleyns School

The Head

On Monday, Edgar Gonfrum said
'I think I'll find another head.
His head was bad, for all his life,
He could not find a loving wife.

On Tuesday, Edgar Gonfrum went
To the town of Stoke-on-Trent.
He tried to find a handsome stone
That he could wear and call his own.

On Wednesday, Edgar Gonfrum saw
A basket held by a man so poor
In the basket was a handsome stone
That he could wear and call his own.

On Thursday, Edgar followed home
The poor old man with the handsome stone.
Little did young Edgar know
Into the river the stone would go.

On Friday, Edgar Gonfrum saw
The stone get thrown by the man so poor
Into the river, Edgar dived
And got the stone and went home to dry.

On Saturday, Edgar Gonfrum wore
The stone he got from the man so poor.
At once the women flocked to him
And told him he looked like a king.

On Sunday, Edgar Gonfrum did wed
A lady with a perfect head
He had twelve children with his wife
And lived a happy untroubled life.

Gabriel Blaazer (11)
Alleyns School

If You Kiss Me

If you kiss me
I shall suffer,
For beneath your lips
A secret burns
So deep and far
Too much for me to handle.
Glinting in your eyes
Concealed in the curl of your smile
Veiled in the tilt of your head.

I want our lips to touch
And pass on mutual sweetness,
But this cannot be;
For every second that passes
On glow your tinted cherry lips
Pulsating and brutal.
Wanting to cause pain.
An emotional twinge.
A shock to the heart.

Honesty lies not here.
You are unaware
Yet still possess a capability
A chance to sense
And a life to spark.

I want our lips to meet
Our shades of reds to fuse,
A tingle to ripple between us.

I want us to fall in love.

Lisa Blair (17)
Alleyns School

I Would Like . . .

I would like to hear
The sound of my pupils
As they penetrate the dark.

I would like to touch
The thoughts of the man in the moon
A silent watchman who guards
His carefree children.

I would like to smell
The air as it whistles
Through my hazel hair
On a billowing, chilly day.

I would like to taste
The soft candyfloss of
The sticky, fluffy clouds.

I would like to see
The sound of my heart
As it pumps energy
Around my body.

I would like to paint
The sun as it drifts dreamily
Up into the cloudless sky.

I would like to reach out and
Wipe the sweat off
Jesus' brow as He carries His crucifix.

Sophia Battle (11)
Alleyns School

War

Stupid war
Why did it ever start?
It's such a bore
All men have to take part
I had to leave
My country and my friends
I couldn't breathe
I had to go so quick I left round the bends
It took ages
I read my book
I got through a million pages
Before I had had a look
Ireland was sunny
There was wildlife
Like a little bunny
And antelopes with funny strife,
War, war, war,
Why can't I be at home?
Bore, bore, bore,
Or in somewhere else like Rome.

Bethany Garratt (11)
Alleyns School

A Fountain Pen

You are old and wise,
Like an old man.
You are dented, yet friendly,
Like an old man.
You are used and familiar,
Like an old man.

You are faded and reliable,
Like an old man.
You are ink-stained, but comforting,
Like an old scholar.
You are mine,
Like my old man.

You are sometimes sly and sometimes stubborn,
Like an old grandfather.
You stain fingers and cry to be used,
Like an ageing scholar.
You are my friend,
Just like my old and ageing grandfather.

Shura Harris (11)
Alleyns School

Vegetables

Vegetables are disgusting horrible things that bring dread
To every meal,
I ate, and I ate, and I ate, and I ate but my greens still sat at
The edge of my plate.

I would rather swim with a great white shark,
Be eaten by dinosaurs sitting in the park,
Play chess with a man-eating rattlesnake,
Than touch those tomatoes that are on my plate.

I'd rather be hit by a monkey's mango,
Be beaten up by a zebra doing the tango,
Have to learn Latin with an inquisitive parrot,
Than eat some peas or even a carrot.

I'd rather play tag with an angry bear,
Wear a rhino's underwear,
Be bitten by a ten foot croc.

Actually I wouldn't.

Adam Broadbent (11)
Alleyns School

My Poem

Her nose upturned, head held high,
Her hair pulled tight on her head,
In a bun.
Overwhelmed by vanity,
She sits with pride,
Her bottom thrust out behind her.

When the time is right,
She lets out a *scream!*
A shrill, piercing note,
From her spotless spout,
She emits steam,
To show that she is ready.

She's clean and neat, and perfect,
The best dressed on the table.
The spoons can clang, the clocks can chime,
But only she can look so fine.

And yet she's just a teapot.

Arianna Sorba (11)
Alleyns School

My Bent Homework

I wish you'll take note,
Cos no one will,
It ate my dad's goat,
And crushed my pills.

I woke up one day with cheese on my face,
(Which beyond doubt put me off),
I opened my mouth and had a taste,
And began to contagiously cough.

My sister dashed in as she madly screamed,
On her hand was a lifeless bird,
Mother came in and sis got creamed,
'Cos the whole neighbourhood had heard!

I knew it just then who the suspect was,
All big beady eyes were on me,
'Raze that plague without an awful fuss,
And remove that rank smell of cheese.'

So when I hauled myself inside the grounds,
I heard a whopping hubbub,
Someone shouted, 'Look what I found!'
And I thought I felt a brush.

There was my work, which stared at me
And was smothered in horrific stains,
But it did something we'd all agree,
It ate the school; I can't complain!

Kevin Co (12)
Alleyns School

The Snowdrop

The snowdrop,
As pure white as the new moon in the ink-black sky.
Each petal crafted to perfection,
Each leaf arranged with love.

He stands upright,
But not in pride.
He hangs his head in shame.
Even when the morning dew settles, glistening on his pale face.

Unique in his own little ways,
But still, just as shy, as the millions of others around him.
A lonely wanderer hidden, amongst a crowd.

Day after day he watches the same blade of grass, gently
swaying as the soft breeze caresses the snowdrop's only company.
Until his leaves begin to droop.

He listens intently to the approaching children's shouts,
Knowing he has little time, knowing what is coming.
He wishes his farewells to the surrounds he has grown accustomed to.

And he asks himself – as the shouts grow louder.
Why was he placed upon this Earth?

Nobody heard his cries of agony as he was trampled beneath
uncaring feet.

Elinor Davis (11)
Alleyns School

The Cat

I stalked around the house
Listening to the giants plodding about upstairs
I lapped up a white, moist liquid
I went through the cat flap into the open air
It was freezing and as silent as space.

Suddenly I heard a rustling in the bushes
My ears pricked up and I crept a little closer
It was another cat
In my territory, how dare he?
I crouched down and hid in the long grass.

It was time to make my move
I jumped up, paws astray
But he was too quick and got me, just above the eye
It stung badly and I was blinded for a split second
I retreated through the cat flap.

I prowled into the big room and leapt onto the sofa
One of the giants was there quietly reading.
I crawled up and climbed onto it
I curled up and was lovingly stroked by the smallest giant
Now was the purrfect time for a cat nap!

Jack Trewin (11)
Alleyns School

Supermarket Cows

Aisles of scarlet, gold and cream
Flashes of ghosts, herded to reap
Bloodied and butchered, now packaged and clean
Stacked and shelved in the old ghosts keep.

Sterile smiles and rambling voices
Medicinal whites float through the aisles
Mumbling mothers burdened with choices
Are eyed from behind by the bovine piles.

Gormless they wander, the old with the young
To queue for the chance to plunder the land
Of watercolour farms buried in dung
Of life sown and reaped by the same sweaty hands.

Silent they queue as if for the butcher
Déjà vu for the phantoms behind
Then smacking their chops they race for the cooker
Speeding their cars with the phantoms inside.

Settled for dinner, the family meal
They prey, polite, impatience in mind
Herds of cattle, collected and spectral
Graze in their garden and wince as they grind.

Rachel Dear (16)
Alleyns School

Hallowe'en

I was ever so excited,
I had reason to be:
We were going to the shops
To buy a pumpkin for me.

I chose a really large pumpkin,
The biggest I could see.
It was as round as the moon,
Mum carried it home for me.

I was back just in time for supper.

I pricked out the face's outline,
On my pumpkin named 'Bea'
Dug out the seeds with Dad's spade,
The scary smile frightened me.

I trick or treated with my mum,
Spooking all I could see,
It was my new witch's mask,
Nobody knew it was me.

I can't wait 'til next year!

Alex De Salis (13)
Alleyns School

Sorrow

Sorrow is the stillborn child,
Never had a chance to smile,
Dead before he could have lived,
Who knows what he had to give?

Sorrow is the broken heart,
No date in a horse-drawn cart,
No romantic honeymoon,
Left with no eternal boon.

Sorrow is the orphan boy,
No parents to give him joy,
No siblings to help him out,
Money he was left without.

Sorrow is the poverty,
Some people don't reach thirty,
All because they're moneyless,
People cannot do their best.

Sorrow isn't the end of hope,
Don't just think you cannot cope,
It'll be all right tomorrow,
Let us bring an end to sorrow.

Alexei Hartley (12)
Alleyns School

The Camera

The camera never lies or so they say.
Some people use one every day.
The flash of a camera like the blink of an eye,
The hooded lens waiting to spy.

The tired old phrase may not be true,
Because now people can digitise you.
The use of computers to tweak the picture
Now make manufacturers richer and richer.

The digital age is at a high,
Traditional photography is going to die.
No more developing, in a darkened room,
Is plunging the camera to its eternal doom.

Real photography is coming to a close,
More and more people are starting to pose.
We are getting rid of a noble art,
It is times like these that sting my heart.

Tradition has to lose, even though it's sad
This will make our ancestors even more mad.
We're not photographing stills like our grandfather,
Now we find ourselves in a digital lather.

Felix de Grey (12)
Alleyns School

The Apocalypse

The sky is darkened overhead
Black clouds hunt the sun
The light is gone from all the world
No one here to see the end

Bucketful after bucketful
Of rain comes coursing down
Thunder's drum roll sounds again
Waterfalls of light race down to smash the earth.

Heaven opens, down they come
Great armies causing great destruction
Scaling walls with grappling hooks
Lurking in every nook and cranny.

A battleaxe comes to strike,
To break the Earth in two.
Volcanoes light up all the land,
Like a massive fire it rages down.

After one almighty bang,
The Earth is gone.
And then, with a mighty ping
The Earth is back, it's all a dream.

Jonathan Anderson (11)
Alleyns School

Alone In A Crowd

Why do you think it doesn't hurt,
When you look at me that way?
I cannot run but I can hear and see,
But maybe I'll walk some day.

Please treat me the same as everyone else,
I am a person just like you.
Don't point and stare and call me names,
My feelings for this are true.

Being different isn't special
Being different isn't wrong.
So why do I feel out of place,
My feelings for this are strong.

Although my arms and legs don't work,
I'm the same as you inside.
Don't look away or patronise,
My feelings I just can't hide.

I love my life and even though,
I'm not the same as you.
OK I'm different I'll admit,
But I'm happy through and through.

Sophie Richardson (12)
Alleyns School

My Bird

My bird flies effortlessly through the summer skies,
So light, so free, so high.
The sun is setting,
Shining in his eyes,
A golden yellow colour,
Raging like a fire.
His feathers soaked in liquid gold,
Shimmer as they flap,
Closer to the glittering sea, far across the map.
He rests on a branch after days of flight,
Shielding his eyes,
Blocking the light.
Other birds chuckle,
Other birds squawk,
But his silent bill does not talk.
Their pointed beaks,
Help them to speak,
To their fellow birds,
In whistle words.
The sun falls down gently,
As do the birds,
But my little bird,
Flies after the sun . . .

Amy Ooi (11)
Alleyns School

The Dancing Tree

Look around, what do you see?
A beautiful landscape? That indeed,
Chimney tops in eyes' way,
Aeroplanes before your face
Makes pollution in every place.

Music booms from a window
Makes the tree dance the limbo.
He sways to the music to and fro
The birds in his branches start to crow.

People walking in the town
See the tree and start to frown
Little children point and stare
Then he shakes his branches bare.

But wait, don't go
There is more to know
The tree was once like me
With thoughts and fears throughout the years
But now he's just a tree.

Emma Waldegrave (11)
Alleyns School

The Cat

It sits at night,
Watching and waiting,
Occasionally moving its paw slowly,
Its movement is lazy,
A car goes past,
It jumps to its feet,
And disappears out the back door.

It stands in the moonlight,
Staring at the stars,
Wishing it was as high,
As high as the clouds and the tops of trees,
Flying as free as a bird in the breeze,
There is a tear in its eye,
And the cat runs away.

Next evening it goes to stroll,
Or for an evening meal,
And then later on it looks at the stars again,
It has a tear in its eye,
And then it lays down to die.

Edward Hawkins (11)
Alleyns School

Beauty

Beauty has lips that shine
Like roses of gold

Skin that's as soft
As an angel's wing

A body that's shaped
From the hands of God

Hair that's as sleek as
A unicorn's mane

Hands that are as delicate
As an orchid's flower

Eyes that are as bright as the
White light of Heaven

A smile that's as beautiful
As creation itself

But where does beauty reside
On the outside or
In the inside?

Alexander Osborne (12)
Alleyns School

To Russia With Love

Dear Mothers of Beslan

As I was clearing up my children's breakfast,
I thought of them happily playing at school,
I heard more on the radio of the terror in Beslan,
Of the killings and the numbers of bodies brought out.

As I was washing my children's clothes,
I pictured how full of life they always are,
I switched on the TV and saw pictures of death,
And heard of children being shot in the back as they fled.

While I'm collecting my children from their school,
I think of you frantically searching for yours,
Searching, among the many dead. The many dead.
I realise how very, very lucky I am, to find mine.

With all my love to you mothers, of School Number One.

Peter Hanton (13)
Alleyns School

Imagine

Imagine you're on the beach
With no one around,
Just yourself,
With the waves crashing against the sand.

Imagine you're in a car,
Stuck in loads of traffic,
Breathing in all the congestion,
With the ground full of tar.

Which one would you choose?

Joseph Corcoran (12)
Bishop Challoner Catholic Collegiate School

Homework

I love homework,
It is cool,
English, maths and science too,
When I do my homework,
I get credits,
It helps me at school,
And it always helps me too.
I wish one day
That I could go away,
To a land with lots of homework,
So then I could get lots of credits,
And get a good grade at school,
Next time I wonder what I could do!

Solomon Adeyi (12)
Bishop Challoner Catholic Collegiate School

My Favourite Sport Is . . .

My favourite sport has people running and jumping
And running and throwing
And so far this might help you knowing
What it is that this sport is.
I'll give you a clue
It begins with 'A'
Could it be aeroball?
Or could it be athletics?
Pick your guess A or B for the day
I'll give you a hint it has a 4x1 relay!

Carl Letang (13)
Bishop Challoner Catholic Collegiate School

Feelings

I feel left out, no one wants to know
No one even cares, no one thinks I'm there
No one takes any notice
Feels like I'm all alone
Feels like no one is around
All alone in the park
Where is everyone?
No one to talk to
No one needs me
Who is there? No one.

I don't feel left out, everyone wants to know
Everyone cares, everyone thinks I'm there.
Everyone takes notice
Feel no longer alone in the park
Where is everyone? Right here
Everyone to talk to
Everyone needs me
Who is there? Everyone!

Jamie Curtis (12)
Bishop Challoner Catholic Collegiate School

Flying

Spreading wings
                And falling,
Gliding, then flapping
                Searching,
Swooping and stalking
                Grabbing
Then flapping and
                Looping,
To a soft landing.

The owl has caught his prey.

Lyndon Morris (12)
Bishop Challoner Catholic Collegiate School

Untitled

I lay by the track
Fearing my death
Staring into coldness
The wire falls down
Slowly, towards me.

It inches so close
Right up to my throat
Then the illusion is gone
I wake from the dream
But have I?

I am in a cornfield
A dusky scene
The surrounding darkness
The evil inside
Crawling, crawling.

Is this a reality?
I do not know
My life, is it a dream?
I must know
But for now
I sleep.

Charlie Holdsworth (15)
Bishop Challoner Catholic Collegiate School

Me

I am one of a kind
        With a confused and challenging mind.

I hate cold weather, it makes me feel cold
        Even though I'm big and bold.

My mum is the best,
        She's better than all the rest.

I am one of a kind
        With a confused and challenging mind.

Freddie Amponsah (12)
Bishop Challoner Catholic Collegiate School

Waiting?

I am a book
Waiting to get read
Pages and pages
I am the one.

I am the one
Left out
On my own
I am the one.

Sometimes
I have friends
Most of the time
They're gone
I am the one

Will I ever get read?

Thomas Mallia (12)
Bishop Challoner Catholic Collegiate School

Crooks

My name is Crooks
I am black
Nobody talks to me
Because I am black
I am well educated
I have loads of books
I am not allowed in the bunkhouse
Because I am black
If I was white
I would get respect
But no I am black.

Christian Antoine-Bryan (14)
Bishop Challoner Catholic Collegiate School

The Dog Who Ate Everything

This dog ate everything
You'll say he never bites
My friends will never knock for me
He'll give them a fright.
When the door opens he runs straight out
And won't come back until he hears me shout.
One day he ate my coat, my hat and even my shoe
I wonder why he does this?
I just do not have a clue.
He eats his food very, very quick,
And when he is finished, just to say thank you
He will give you a lick
Why is this dog so lively?
I really do not know.

Leeson McDowell (12)
Bishop Challoner Catholic Collegiate School

One Metre Tent

There was an irritating spider
That was climbing up my wall,
The second I tried to hit it
It ran halfway down the hall.
On and on this spider went
It even climbed over my one metre tent!
I turn my attention to a buzzing bee
Hold on there's a herd of spiders heading for me!
On and on I went
Is it safe in this one metre tent?

Ife Aderoba (12)
Bishop Challoner Catholic Collegiate School

Natural World

In the natural world
All the flowers different colours
Red, blue, purple and yellow
All these different colours
Which one should I pick?
The red flower reminds me of rosy cheeks
The blue flower reminds me of the sky and the sea
The purple flower reminds me of a bunch of grapes
The yellow flower reminds me of the sun and the sand
They are all so colourful
I still don't know which one to pick
I might pick one, I might pick all of them
And that is what I will do
I will pick all of them.

Jason Stefano (12)
Bishop Challoner Catholic Collegiate School

Autumn

The leaves on the trees are crispy and red
Frosty mornings, the leaves are falling,
Roadsides full with crispy leaves,
Car windows frosted up,
Birds whistling, please come outside
You don't know what you are missing
You can smell the fresh autumn morning.
It makes me feel so relaxed even though I'm cold.
I feel fresh because the air is fresh
That's why I feel autumn is the best month.

Kane Lyons (12)
Bishop Challoner Catholic Collegiate School

Untitled

Life's but walking shadows, everywhere you go
You'll see destruction, hate, sadness, racism, attitudes
And prejudice.
One day the world will become an end,
When it comes to an end you'll see the world come apart
And people will come apart.
Need the world to be strong then listen; everybody's different.
No two people in the world are the same. It is important
To remember this
People have different races, ages, religions, cultures, skin colours, eye
colour, hair colour, size, disabilities and attitudes are all different.
All people are equal!
Everyone deserves equal respect.
That's why life is but a walking shadow.

Rizwan Mohammed (14)
Bishop Challoner Catholic Collegiate School

Me And The City

Me and the city
Where the towers are tall
They look at me in a fine way, saying don't worry
We'll guide the way from the bad and good.
I love the city
The city loves me
So feel happy
When you're in the city
The bad is gone.
So come on in,
The towers will guide you safely
So don't be afraid from the city come on in.

Albert Cooper (12)
Bishop Challoner Catholic Collegiate School

Untitled

The paper is blank,
So is my mind,
Sitting outside,
Watching a skater do a grind.

What a great skill,
I continue to think,
There's a girl in the background,
Who gave me a wink.

I look down at the paper,
It's still blank like a forehead of horizontal wrinkles,
I don't know what to do,
My mind just rolls over, over, over.

The girl walked over,
Sat down beside me,
She asked for my name,
My mind went blurry.

Her name in my mind,
My name in the girl's,
She's the girl of my dreams,
Her hair blonde and in curls.

Barrie Gable-Williams (14)
Bishop Challoner Catholic Collegiate School

Basketball

My name is Kenny Afrifa and I love to play basketball,
I'm a very good player even though I'm not so tall.

People think that they can take advantage of me,
But step on the court, they will see.

Basketball is as precious as a wife
As precious as gold, as precious as my life.

So if anyone out there is looking for a game
Meet me on the court and you will feel the shame.

Kenny Afrifa (12)
Bishop Challoner Catholic Collegiate School

Wilderness

In a rainforest
Lives a beast
Unknown to man.

With its black fur,
It hides in the
Shadows.

It has eyes of
Cold yellow steel
And if you get
Too close you'll be a meal.

Jumping tree to tree
It slowly hunts its
Prey.

Is it a lion, a bear
Or tiger what would
    It be?

Nobody knows what
It is but do you
Know what it is?

Shane Tivnan (12)
Bishop Challoner Catholic Collegiate School

Sleeping

When I drift asleep
I hear the black birds
Sing around my dreamy
Head but to my surprise
On my suntanned brow comes
Drumming rain to spoil my
Gentle sweet dream.

Jack Georgiou (14)
Bishop Challoner Catholic Collegiate School

The Wrong Turning

I walk about, I watch my back
'Cause I might get stabbed or savagely attacked.
I think to myself why live this way
It's cause I took the wrong turning back in the day.
I used to be good but I turned bad
Just cause I wanted to be Jack the lad.
It might sound stupid but it's really sad
That wrong turn has made me mad.

I used to be good at school, I was a normal child
But a couple of turnings later I turned out to be wild.
And then one more thing I would like to say
Don't take the wrong turning, go the right way.

Tony Shaughnessy (14)
Bishop Challoner Catholic Collegiate School

Of Mice And Men

(Inspired by 'Of Mice And Men' by John Steinbeck)

Lennie, Lennie, stop that Lennie
Lennie, Lennie put that back
Don't forget this, don't forget that.
Now he's killed this, now he's killed that
Help me, help me, oh Clara help me
Stay away from this, stay away from that
A piece of land here, a piece of land there,
All I hear is alafa, rabbits, alafa, rabbits
I could be town, I could be town
But no not me, if only, if only . . .

Stefan Regis (14)
Bishop Challoner Catholic Collegiate School

Samurai

With katana in hand,
They cleanse the land,
Loyalty unmatched,
They battle with faith unscratched,
They know no fear,
When their foe is near,
Their holy creed,
Their faith's true seed.
In their hearts only honour
Their death is never true,
Japan their native land,
They protect it through and through,
With the guidance of God's hand!

Dean Currie (14)
Bishop Challoner Catholic Collegiate School

The Decision

(Inspired by 'Of Mice And Men' by John Steinbeck)

I knew in my head that this time would come
This brainless buffoon has done it again.
He's done it in Weed and now in Soledad.
He does not mean to do it.
But he has no control.

He likes to pet and play with soft things.
I knew this time would come,
Now, why is it me to end it all for him?

Got to keep him happy, it's the last seconds of his life
Because I'm about to end it all for him . . .

Kadeem Douglas (15)
Bishop Challoner Catholic Collegiate School

Time

Time seeps through our fingers like an eel
Will we truly be remembered for what we've done.
Or what we haven't.
What we lose is lost forever
And nothing we do can stop that.
What's done is done.
What's done is done.
Time will always be one step ahead.
What's done is done
Is time an illusion?
What's done is done
Is it just a state of mind?
What's done is done
Is what we've lost, lost forever?
What's done is done,
Has it an end?
What's done is done.

Paul Aylett (14)
Bishop Challoner Catholic Collegiate School

D-Day Poet

My D-Day poem is a poem of truth,
D-Day was a day of death,
D-Day when a lot of faithful men took their last breath,
D-Day was a day of victory and of loss,
Too many people were lost,
Half the people didn't want to be there,
Plus some people don't even care,
How can you say a day like that was a day of victory or glory?
D-Day; a day of liberation.
A day of victory it was not!

James Falzon (14)
Bishop Challoner Catholic Collegiate School

Friends

(Inspired by 'Of Mice And Men' by John Steinbeck)

There are two men
That are best friends.
In a lonely town
Everyone seems to be lonely
Except them.
George is a caring man looking after his friend
When he doesn't have to.
Lennie is not a simple man,
He's a man, but not in the head
He's a big lovely caring man
But doesn't know how to control himself.

They are both in a world that
Is depressed and alone
People are looking at them as if they are aliens
Because in this world no one looks after anyone's back
It's everyone for themselves.

And because of this lack of self control
Lennie kills a woman and then George has to
Put a gun to Lennie's head.
Then he shoots from behind rather than
Let the others torture his friend,
But it kills George inside to do it.

Kieren George (14)
Bishop Challoner Catholic Collegiate School

Poets

Astrologers know about planets
Writers about words
Philosophers know about thought
And Bill Oddie about birds
Pilots know about flying
Through the skies up above
Bankers may know about money and things
But poets have the knowledge of love.

Serena Manteghi (16)
Hampstead School

The End Of The Road

She looks at his blurred face,
Knowing she won't last this life-long race,
He looks back at her with a reassuring smile,
She can see his face a little clearly now.

'Go to sleep,' he says, 'I'll still be here,'
She closes her eyes and overcomes her fear,
Soaring through the multicoloured sky,
Waving and smiling at the passers-by.

She rises higher into the weightless clouds,
Appreciating every smell and sound,
Feeling the soft touch of the cool breeze,
Never, ever wanting to leave.

Floating outside a golden gate,
Upholding her doomed fate,
Her eyes begin to water again,
Feeling the most overwhelming pain.

'Come in,' said a deep voice,
And soon all she heard was noise,
She saw her ancestors; she was safe,
This would be her resting place.

The heart monitor went wild,
Her father howled and cried,
'Goodbye my child, I love you with all my heart,'
He held her hand until it was time for them to part.

He kissed her cold forehead,
And left his only daughter in a hospital bed,
He walked out and closed the door behind him,
And waited for the day they would be reunited.

Leanne Chorekdjian (14)
Hampstead School

One War, One Thousand Tears

I ran and I ran as fast as I could.
I didn't know where I was going,
I didn't even know if I could.

Bombs were going off everywhere, wounded children
Laying down in despair.
Lives lost, one or the other.
Every family trying to find each other.

I wished to find mine, I wished for the war to stop.
I saw a man laying dead on the floor,
The gun shooting at him raged a big pop.

Dead people in all places and everyone with shocked faces.
I could never have seen anything worse,
It seemed all the people were somewhat cursed.

Everyone was in such fear, and myself, I shed my tear.
One tear for the war and for the people.
Some of them will soon be at the steeple.

But then I asked myself a rhetorical question,
Hoping bombs would be going off in a different direction.
Some people have travelled through our horrific world.
The sadness they went through, the traumatic hell.

I thank something higher that I'm not a refugee,
But some are either a he or a she.
I don't know how I got to this place in heart,
But to go through this I am sure many people can't.

Scarlet Fallon-O'Sullivan (13)
Hampstead School

Live Or Die?

This is the day I die
My very face just a shadow in your mind
My very being gone
This will be the day I die.

I have lied and I have cheated and I have been very rude,
But now I'm gone and no tears to be shed.
No one's to cry
No one's to weep
As I will be there
Maybe at my funeral
Maybe at my mass
Because I'm always there
Dead or alive
I have lied and I do care
But I will die today
My body and shell has gone
But my mind and soul will for ever live on.

On the other hand have I really died?
If I'm not gone and my soul still lives on
Then have I really gone?
Did I really die
Or did I just lie?
I went to my mass
And saw all my mates
But they didn't see me
They had a sad face.

Gemma Ross (13)
Hampstead School

Poetry

'A quality that pleases the mind, as poetry does'

Yet who decides what makes a good poem?
Poet, public, or poetry plural
Do they sit by each other
Comparing size or intellectuality?
Or is it when a pure expression of oneself
Is animated, on a previously blank page?

Is it a single word
Comprised of six to ten letters
Coupled with a noun, adjective or verb
Or is it a feeling?
A momentary lapse of cold clinical thought,
Which clutches at the heart
Causing it to quicken
Dancing, for even one unique second.

Can a poem change life
Or is it destined to lie glued to a page?
Read only by people who happen to stumble on its number,
In a book of its rivals
On which it always must compete,
To stay remembered.

Or will people study it
Discovering things which were never there
Stripping it naked, under cold, hard student glare
Scalpel replaced with a bright red marker pen
Leaving it just some ink staining a page.
People will never let beauty be what it is.
Itself.

Ander Fraser (16)
Hampstead School

Willow Is Not For Everyone

(Inspired by 'Elm' by Sylvia Plath)

I weep, she says, 'You cannot
See my tears
How they slip freely to the floor.'

'You know the ground,' she says, 'I do not,
I am only shallow, expect nothing,
My roots are slender.

My tresses curl and intertwine
Look. They form an eye
See how it gazes at you, infinite, beauty.

My leaves are sleek, streamlined,
You are gnarled. Nothing to offer.
Try not to expect too much.

You're rotten now, so they tell me?
Listen. It's getting worse,
You can hear them whispering.'

Shhh. Shhh. They say,
They could cut it out,
Extract your contamination.

But he reaches out and touches me
Golden fingertips caress my face, leaves, skin,
Only darkness smiles upon you.

He won't look at you, I am his shrine
His regard will disregard your place
And look upon mine.

Because the words fell like decaying leaves,
What a nightmare. Forget it. Forget it.
Meaningless, it burns like fire.

The wind is whispering in my ear
The wind is growing
Your defiance builds but –

Hush do you hear them?
Footsteps clear the darkness of love,
Coming to cut you.

Thump Thump. Tresses slip in clumps. Matted.
All is still. Sap seeps like blood.
They kill, yes they kill. They kill.

Shireen Qureshi (16)
Hampstead School

Caged Kid

Here I am, stuck in the society
Hoping one day, be great in the industry
I'll travel around, country to country
My dreams will be ruined with me being unhappy.

I hide from those, who assume priority
There's no need, for me to have popularity
But it makes all the difference, I can guarantee
I always want to hide my identity
And stay treated as though I am charity
It's as if I'm a refugee
But it's better than those who are unfair to me.

I'm sick of being that quiet tree
Shrunk to the size of a tiny green pea
All I ever want to see
Is me, being happy and free.

Alex Nqai (13)
Hampstead School

Mine

Silence.
Who am I?
No one, a figment.
Sometimes I'm just not here.
So who am I?
Cynical, tired, insecure.
A misfit.
I'm not yours.

Extraordinary, how you've managed
To never really see me,
But still have judged me.
So tell me what you see.
I'm everything you're not
And I don't need you.
But somehow I still find myself
Waiting for your approval.

I'm just one of those faces
You pass by.
But I am here.
I am alive,
Can't you hear me screaming
And can't you hear me crying?
I wish that for once someone
Would just see me
For who I really am.

And I apologise
For this intrusion.
Your ignorant life was never meant
To be tainted by my disapproval.
I should just keep this to myself
Silently bitter.
And I despise you for thinking everything
Is so perfect.

Me?
I am what you don't understand.
I am myself and somewhere inside of me
I know that I am so much more.
So forget all of this.
For I am not yours,
I am mine, and
I see me.

Kitty Jenkins (16)
Hampstead School

I Bought My Mum An Apple

I bought my mum an apple,
But it wasn't red or green.
It was more like bluish-purple,
Or some colour in-between.

I wouldn't call the blueberries,
I bought her very blue.
They were rather reddish-orange,
Like a dark vermilion hue.

The oranges I got for her,
Weren't as orange as you'd think.
They were turquoise on the inside,
And the outer peels were pink.

The strawberries I purchased,
Weren't particularly red.
They were white with purple polka dots,
And silver stripes instead.

I got all these by shopping,
Where I'd never shopped before.
That's the last time I buy groceries,
At the Rainbow grocery store!

Lilybeth King (13)
Hampstead School

Man

He is so many things
His self is everything
'I will bring home the fire'
He says.

No worries are ever used in him
They will only be wasted.

Himself to his woman
Is like
A father to his daughter
A lizard to its rock
The land to the ocean.

I want to love him
I do so much
But my frail love and affection
Cannot penetrate
Within the tough, muscular walls of himself
The true beauty of man and woman together
Is the contrast
The contrast between them
Weakness and strength
Fear and courage
Calm and rage
Exposition and protection.

But the man is the true beauty
I live for him
He lives for me
He saves me
It's wondrous
That he was made from the weakness of a mother
And her minuteness
Whereas he is sheer thick muscle
And bone.

We leave the man
With his tiny lady
His diminutive, yet
Enormous reason to live
His intimidating, yet whole-like
Harmless self
Engulfs his love inside
His invincible torso

Tonight

Tomorrow
He entombs
Me.

Maxine Ellah (14)
Hampstead School

All I Really Want To Do . . .

I awake by the screeching beep
But all I really want to do is sleep
I pull on my clothes with no delight
When five minutes ago I was as high as a kite.

And as I tame the beast with my brush
All I can do is daydream about my crush
I'm almost awake as I splash water on my face
I look at the clock, I have to pick up the pace.

I sit to eat breakfast while I listen to Bam Bam
As he tells me about the M1 traffic jam
As well as him there is also Street Boy
Who acts like a kid with a new toy.

I'm ready now out the door I go
To school where I see my friends and co
I sit in history and hear how the world is so deep
But in my head all I really want to do is sleep.

Terri Morris (16)
Hampstead School

A Gift, A Curse Of Each Day To Come

The conflict of my life, is full of sore clichés,
I dance around each minute and sing away the days.

A message embedded in my head is too blurry to see,
I don't know what day it is and I can't find my keys.

Ten hours of TV watching seems the logical thing to do,
But I'm tired and I don't want to go to sleep; I really don't have a clue.
I sat on a wall yesterday and gazed at this flower shop,
My heart ached so much as the petals began to drop.

I stare into space as I lie on my bed and throw a tennis ball
At the ceiling,
Each bounce is my pulse fading away;
I need a new day, I need healing.

A silence falls in each in-between,
When the fairies come out and the world turns green.

The clouds are birthmarks of where love has been present,
And rain is the heartbreak that shows in each crescent.

And in the midnight hour, when story shadows are cast,
I'll breathe in all those minutes and days,
Knowing they won't be my last.

Leah Devlin (14)
Hampstead School

Subliminal Lies

Subliminal lies try to steer our lives,
Control what we think or say,
Messages hidden around us,
Everywhere it seems,
Everyone's affected, reflecting what they see
And through the time I write this rhyme,
They're thinking of how to use new finds,
To tell us what we should buy next,
All enclosed in their advert's text.

Nicholas Courtman (13)
Hampstead School

Thoughts Of Tuesday

Out of the window
The sky is blue
And clear
It's deceiving
I put an umbrella in my bag.

I mute the TV
Deciding that to write poetry
I need to concentrate.
The flickering screen
Tugged at my mind
A soundless soap opera
Maybe I'll leave it till tomorrow.

Anna Robin (16)
Hampstead School

Rose

Red petals shining as bright as the sun,
Look into it and get blind.

As it gets darker, you could still see
The shadow waving about, hear it
Singing happiness all around.

You could hear its vibrating sound
All about, which shines into the dark velvet sky,
When the rose closes down,
Waiting for another adventure to come
While I close my eyes
Imagining another day still to survive.

Fjerza Bekteshi (13)
Hampstead School

Goldfish

You could be a shark
If you really, really wanted to.
All smooth and slick and sharp
If you really, really wanted to.
But to be a shark is not your wish
I know you are, at heart, a goldfish.

You could be a whale
If you really, really wanted to.
All mellow and gentle and frail.
If you really, really wanted to
But to be a whale is not your wish
I know you are, inside, a goldfish.

You could be a trout, a mackerel or a pouting,
A haddock, a plaice, a bream or a whiting.
You could be a conger eel
But I know that that's not how you feel.

I know you are a goldfish,
A goldfish deep inside.
You're charming and you're sweet
And you've got humour you can't hide.
You're a goldfish full stop. That's it.
You're a goldfish and I love you for it.

Lyria Eastley (16)
Hampstead School

Hurt Inside

(Inspired by 'Small Pain In My Chest' by Michael Hack)

A boy lay still on his bed as the evening caressed the sky.
Tears strolled down his cheek as the cars passed by.
His body motionless but his mind couldn't lie.
I did not understand why this boy did cry.

The warmth of his hand on his chest told me he loved someone dear,
That with her undying care, she rid him of all fear,
That no wind could push them from walking by each other's side
And that he would protect her from hurting inside.

The felt-tip heart she drew on his arm,
Told me that within their close hug she felt far from harm,
That the symbol of love filled him with pride,
And that he would protect her from hurting inside.

His parted lips told me they touched with no feeling
That he knew his intentions and that it wasn't his true meaning
That he deceived and lied
In order to protect her from hurting inside.

I looked into his gazing eyes and they told me all
That she couldn't look at him, her name he called . . .
And with that, his heart died,
As he was the one that hurt her inside.

Marcelino Rey (16)
Hampstead School

The Three Witches

The lightning struck down like a judge's hammer,
The storm was worse than the hurricane in Alabama
The wind howled like a wolf under the moon,
This storm didn't look like it was going anywhere soon.
The storm was made by three witches,
Who had made the lightning make three ditches,
They sat round their big black pot,
Last time this had happened they had eaten a baby straight from
                                                    the cot,
They threw in two wolves' eyes and one whole frog,
And yes they got this from a bog,
Four newts and half a rat's tail,
Some off-cheese and some bread that had gone all stale,
Half a monkey and two thirds of a snake,
And also some algae fresh from a lake,
Now they boiled this for about half an hour,
While they waited they watched flower power,
Which if you have ever watched is a gardening programme,
Now if they had gotten it right it should have slightly tasted like ham,
But unfortunately they had forgotten one ingredient
        You!

Oscar McLaughlin (13)
Hampstead School

Soul Innocence

I sit here and flick the switch and see a quiet lonely
Soul picking up her shattered pieces of confidence
Skewn across the brightly coloured truck.

'I just wanted to inform you dearest, that your
daughter's hair is very close to absurd.'

I sit here and flick the switch and see a young soul
Blinded and safeguarded from the truth of a real world.

'Do not look' – He made it clear.
It was a dead body.

I sit here and flick the switch on and see a confused soul,
Saddened and mesmerised of what is behind
This vast curtain.

'Why did not one, not even one, think to stop or help?'
Blood on our conscience.

I sit here and flick the switch and I am tempted to see a lonely,
Saddened, violent person, breathing and sleeping around me;
My own conscience
Like that young soul.

Do you also see the tiny ray of a long forgotten and lost innocence?
Your innocence.

Iyanu Taiwo (16)
Hampstead School

Story Of A Yearning Heart

Every hour of the day that I think of you,
I reminisce of the things we did when we were together . . .
When I looked into your deep brown eyes, I found myself
Lost in a new world
One that I thought could never be taken from me
You made me feel different, a new kind of high
A feeling so sensual just the sight of you
Would make me fuzzy inside,
Then the day I never thought would come,
Things around me began to crumble and everything
Was taken away from me . . .
Now to see you every day knowing you aren't mine
Still for some reason it hurts me deep down inside
I never thought someone could ever do this to me,
Make me feel this way yet they hurt me when they went away.
My heart still cries and my lips yearn for that tender kiss,
Yet I may never tell you the way I feel,
The fact I want you so bad and it will never happen
So now I will love you from afar and live with the fact
My heart forever yearns for your beauty.

Quaam Animashaun (16)
Hampstead School

None

For everything there must come a last.
A last minute, a last hour, a last month, day or year.
A last drink, a last coke, a last beer, whiskey or water.
A last love, a last heart, a last kiss, hug, or rage . . .
Or even the last words written on a page.
But the worst last thing is your last breath
Because what is to follow will assuredly be your death.

Thomas Petrie (14)
Hampstead School

History

Here I'm told to write a poem
To write a piece of history
And as I search for inspiration
Nothing really comes to me.
I sit and think of love and war
As these are popular examples
I ponder the importance of my poem
Of my little sample.
As that's really all it is
It's a sample of the thoughts of me
Not a masterpiece or a work of art
But like a leaf is to a tree
So here I am, I've written my poem.
It's short, it's loud, it's kinda mad
And in a way, it does show Lauren
As really, truly, very bad.

Lauren Watters (16)
Hampstead School

Poems

Poems aren't what everyone likes,
Not all rhyme,
Or sound alike,
They take awhile to make and write,
Nevertheless, the conclusion isn't always right.
Some are long,
And some are short,
Barely most are intense,
Not all bear passion or affection,
Some sustain hatred and envy,
Glee or grief
Or simply tell a stimulating story,
Under another light.

Tiffany Dowden (13)
Hampstead School

Always There

It is there now
In the back of my head
Pushing itself forward
Growing
A thousand screams at once
Quiet
Only I can hear it.

I laugh
A taste of happiness
I swallow
The taste disappears
It comes back again
Larger than before
Dark
Strangling
I cry
It seizes the opportunity
Help me.

The bitter taste of wine
Forcing it back to its silent corner
Absent
But not for long,
I try
I live
It is always there.

Nora Nilsen (16)
Hampstead School

The Mountain

The mountain stands steady and strong
The ageless face of rock in darkness and light
Life flourishes upon the rock each day and night
It dies and is reborn again.

The mountain stands steady and strong
As water runs swiftly through its veins
The greatest waterfalls feed the many rivers and streams
Which connect the mountain to the sea.

The mountain stands steady and strong
In its great gloomy shadow a town appears
Now its rivers are polluted
And the trees all cut down

The mountain stands steady and strong
But the birds don't sing
But the trees don't whistle in the breeze
And the rivers are not rivers.

The mountain stands steady and strong
Anger perverts its thought
It shakes it upon the land and town
Steam erupts from the peak of ice.

The mountain stands steady and strong
The mountain killed what was left of life upon it
Made the land plain and peaceful
And life began anew.

Alexander Wainstok (13)
Hampstead School

Untitled

'Mirror, mirror, on the wall
Who's the fairest of them all?'
I already know the answer.
My stepdaughter.
That bitch.
There was a time when the mirror loved
Me best.
Before I was usurped by
A younger model.
It's always the way.

I gaze into the mirror:
Lovehandles,
Saggy tits.
I'm 57 and I look it.
Every bit of me old,
Wrinkling;
Gravity's winning this battle.

All day long I look at her
Hate her.
The care her father lavishes on her,
The presents:
I hate her.

The mirror's scathing words
Echo in my head.
Every day I ask it
The same question and
It retorts with
The same answer,
Stirring me into a frenzy.

I wrack my brains for the answer,
Some foolproof way
To outdo her beauty.
I'm sick of being
Second-best.

Kirsty O'Neill (16)
Hampstead School

What's It All About?

What's it all about?

I wake up every day
Try to prepare myself for the day ahead
I wonder what life is all about
How we got here,
Maybe our ancestors came in little spaceships,
From another galaxy
And they decided the bananas tasted better here
Than they did in the Milky Way.

What's it all about?
I wonder why I go to school,
My family tell me, 'So you can get a good job and
                                    Make us proud.'
You know that sort of thing.

What's it all about?
I often depress myself when I think about death.
It's one of those subjects,
It has so many unanswered questions
But you're too scared to ask.
Like, what happens when you die?
Or, why am I so scared about it?
You can never really know what happens,
It's just one of those things,
That you never know the answer to
Until it actually happens.

What's it all about?
To me, the fact is
Death comes to us all, it's inevitable,
But, until then,
I'm going to go with the flow,
See where it takes me.
That's how it has been,
That's how it is,
And that's how it will end.

Jennifer Gildea (13)
Hampstead School

My Early Life

I am thinking of my early age,
When I was born I was in a weak stage.
Almost every child when born,
Are put in a special ward,
And the nurses strongly thought
Take care of the newly born.

After two months of my arrival
The doctors said it is vital,
For our parents to take care,
Of our everyday needs and then,
If anything may go wrong,
Call the ambulance and be strong.

Our parents did their best,
Day and night without rest,
Took care of us in such a style,
Kept our rooms as clean as crystal,
And saved us from sickness
Our little bodies from weakness.

Slowly, slowly we grew up,
The life around us is getting rough
And by the time we realise,
We are teenager guys
And we need to take study seriously,
To be able to pass our GCSEs.

Our parents are getting aged,
But supporting us in every stage
And are hoping that we will make it
All our exams we will pass,
And they will proud of us.

I consider myself lucky,
To have such a good family,
And whenever I ask for something,
They always give us everything,
Tiredness they consider nothing,
And they are always there to help,
God bless them in every step.

Julian Marton (13)
Hampstead School

Beauty

Beauty is yours, to keep and own,
Black white or big boned,
It's your choice, to show it or not,
Beauty is your heart it can't be stopped,
Beauty can be looks or just held inside,
Beauty can be fear and beauty can be pride
Beauty can mean loads of different things,
Beauty can hold you down or give you wings.

I'm saying this because it's a major part of life,
You can get it when you're single, or with a wife,
This is mostly aimed at boys for their lack of beauty,
We all have to show it sometimes, because it is our duty . . .

And that's why I'm writing a poem about beauty.

James Woods-Segura (13)
Hampstead School

Two Men Fighting On The Street

One man grabbing,
The other one crying,
Women shouting,
Others laughing,
Dogs barking
Old women standing,
Thinking . . . *why were they arguing?*
Just two men fighting on the street.

The lady looks back in dismay,
Saying what a bunch of stupid boys,
They must have had too much to drink,
Seeing as they were best of friends.
Just two men fighting on the street.

Tunde Yusuff (11)
Holloway School

Beg For Mercy

(Inspired by 'What Were They Like?' By Denise Levertov)

Dear Lord, if you hear me,
Forgive my sins from today,
Please Lord, hear my plea,
Because I took a life away.

There's blood, on my shirt and I know it ain't mine.
This is blood of a man. A man, who I shot from behind.
With no gun. No knife. Nor weapon in sight.
The man knew of his fate. So he never put up a fight.
Bang!
With one shot, the man, was down
The wife looked at him and didn't make a sound.
She fell on her knees and started crying.
Broken hearted and weeping,
Screaming her last goodbyes as her husband lay dying.

Dear Lord, if you hear me,
Forgive my sins from today,
Please Lord, hear my plea,
Because I took a life away.

As I left that scene, I felt nothing but guilt,
But this pain was nothing, compared to how the wife felt.
I didn't want to shoot him! But, I was ordered to,
I was trying to be a good soldier! Is this what good soldiers do?
Killing, doesn't solve anything, so I don't understand . . .
Was there a point of me killing that poor, innocent man?

War is not the answer, it never is!
I cannot believe now I made it come to this.
So I'll put this gun to my head and hope the Lord will hear my plea,
For all those soldiers who I have killed,
Hell is where you'll find me . . .

Jamal Gayle (15)
Holloway School

Cannot Stand

(Inspired by 'What Were They Like?' by Denise Levertov)

I cannot stand the sound of death
Which seems to come from east and west.
I cannot stand the screams and shouts
Which seem to come from north and south.
I cannot seem to understand
Why God has such a high demand
For the souls of innocent lives
To take a husband from his wife.
To take a woman from her love
To take a child who's done nothing wrong.
I always ask the question why?
Is this the Devil in disguise?
If it's not
I can't understand what made you raise your hand
And with one fatal swing
Take the joys, traditions and songs we sing.
All this in a war of peace!
And in the pages of history it will never be erased.

Oliver Beccles (15)
Holloway School

Homeless

H is for the home I don't have!
O is for opposite, mine's between rich and poor!
M is for money I don't have!
E is for emptiness in my heart!
L is for lonely which I am all the time!
E is for energy I never have!
S is for shocked which I feel about my life!
S is for sorrow for leaving friends and family behind!

Lakaia Chapman (12)
Holloway School

School

The tall blue building
Thousands of children shouting
Hundreds of teachers mumbling
It's in the school.

'Please' 'Sneeze' 'Stop'
'No' 'Yes' 'Pack-up'
The sounds of the school.

School, the beginning of life and success
The beginning and the end.

Half-term!
Children scream, noise pollutes
End of school day.
School transforms into a haunted cemetery,
As quiet as a cemetery.

No children, no teachers.

Daniel Mantey (14)
Holloway School

Untitled

There's a family of four,
Waiting at the airport's door,
The traffic is mad,
Pollution is bad,
But yet, this family ain't sad.
Is that him? Yes it must be,
He's walking up to me,
It's the long-lost son, who got put up for adoption
It wasn't the mum's fault, she never had an option,
But now the family want him back,
So he hands his father his big brown sack.
The tall, tanned young handsome guy
True to his word, won't ever lie,
The mother smothers him with kisses,
The dreams come true, and the mother's wishes.

Ben Kinsella (13)
Holloway School

Two Men

I glared at two men having a fight . . .
They came towards me and it gave me a fright,
So I ran like the speed of light.

I knew they were coming after me . . .
I wish I was a bird flying free.
Their heavy breathing I could hear,
My adrenaline pumping causing me fear,
But what had I done?
Nothing I could see!
Maybe it was something that they disliked about me?
I froze as their footsteps closed in,
Tears welling in my eyes.
And as I tensed, waiting to be caught,
They ran straight past me,
Leaving me in thought . . .

It wasn't me they wanted after all,
I really thought it was me,
That was my belief,
Slowly a smile spread across my face,
It was a smile of pure relief.

Conor Jones (12)
Holloway School

How Does It Feel?

H ungry are you?
O wn opinions
M ean nothing
E veryone is
L onely in some way
E verything
S eems to be different
S eems to be empty.

Dagmawit Amdemichael (13)
Holloway School

I Am At One With Myself

My soul is lost and confused,
It's trying to find me
It wants to be one with me again,
My soul does not want to be alone.

In my mind I am alone,
In this world I am alone
No one there, no one to help me,
In this life of sin.

Life can be beautiful
Life can be horrible
Make the most of your life
Life is precious, live free, die well.

I am happy and joyful
I am at one with my soul
We feel safe and happy together
We can't live without each other.

Ryan Wenzel (13)
Holloway School

Homeless

H is for the heaviness I feel upon my back
O is when I'm overcome with fear
M is for the money I wish was in my pack
E is for everyone I miss so dear
L is for the loneliness that fills me up each day
E is for the endless wishing, wishing I was home
S is for the sadness I feel upon my way
S is for all the strength that keeps me going
    When I'm on my own.

Chloe Hester (12)
Holloway School

Shall We Begin?

'Nurse, let's begin'
'Maybe I should get my nails done, what do you think doctor?'
'This is going to take quite some time.'
'Oh dear, where do you suggest I begin?'
'Scalpel!'
'My friend Betty knows an excellent manicurist, perhaps I
should go and see her, I think I want a maroon colour.'
'Eughh!'
'No?'
'Oh no! The patient is bleeding.'
'You're right, red is not my colour.'
'Arrghh! Tissue, nurse!'
'Bless you doctor.'
'There, almost done.'
'What? I haven't even picked a colour yet.'
'Let's wash up.'
'Shall we begin the operation, doctor?'

Fahima Khan (11)
Islamia Girls' School

Red Rose

Red sheet of silk floats over water
Protective thorns like needles spiking
Palms begin to open
Scattering of soft petals
Like rich raindrops soaring from a waterfall
Velvet feeling prickles down my spine
Like the taste of sweetness
The scent of fineness -
Like a heart filled with love
Like layers of silk
Like a flower from Heaven.

Esma Al-Sibai (11)
Islamia Girls' School

The Ocean

An ocean as cold as fresh blocks of freezing ice.
That would make you melt the instant you touch it.

An ocean as colourful as a magnificent rainbow,
Except in beautiful shades of blue.

An ocean as beautiful as a gleaming turquoise gown
Sparkling as much as the glittering sun.

An ocean moving as graceful as a ballet dancer
Dancing to every beat of music.

An ocean, as vast as the gigantic universe
And as endless as night-time sky.

An ocean is like a plastic carrier bag:
Carrying ships, boats, people and fish.

Nashwa Ali (11)
Islamia Girls' School

Friendship

Not breakable
Not destroyable
Strong as a rock
It can't be changed.

Sweet like candy
Colourful like a rainbow
Happy as a clown
Joyful as me.

Elegant like a swan
Proud as a peacock
To be together all the time.

Friendship will last forever.

Zainab Arshad (11)
Islamia Girls' School

The Rose

I sleep on the bench and I find a rose
I look and stare and see how it glows.

I sit up and hold it with my own hands,
The rose is shining and brings a drift of memories.

This is telling me
How I am lucky to have an admirer
Their lover
Their heart
Like an eagle in the sun
Like a soaring bird in the sky
Like my heart has been held from the sky.

Amina Hassan (11)
Islamia Girls' School

The Deep Blue Sea

Big blue beautiful
Relaxing and exciting
Has salt, who cares?
Jellyfish surrounding us
In the sea fish tickling me
Come and collect shells with me.

Zeynep Tahir (11)
Islamia Girls' School

My Diary

I only have one
Where my secrets are revealed
It has a padlock
Even lots of pages
No one but me uses it.

Ameena Majeed (11)
Islamia Girls' School

The Day I Went To My Friend

The day I went to my friend, well
That day never came to an end,
The way things were going
Well the whole thing was showing.

In the morning when I woke up
I found frozen tea in my cup
And after that
I fell on the cat.

When I went downstairs to my mum
I called Dad for breakfast, but he would not come.

I went up to my room,
When my mum shouted, '*School!*'
Oh what am I going to do?
I think I am getting the flu.

The flu was definitely coming
Because of that very strange humming
I've heard that before
On the very last floor
In the Bentalls Centre Building.

When I went out
To see what all the commotion was all about
I saw my best friend
So this is the end.

Amna Sabih (11)
Islamia Girls' School

Ocean

Like a huge blue cloth
Like a tide with tropic hills
Plaiting hair in waves
Like fields of sparkling diamonds
Turns her material gazes.

Sana Ali (11)
Islamia Girls' School

My Kitten Snowball

I curl around Snowball
As happiness surrounds me
Herds of fur soften me
Love snows down on me.

Pieces of sadness melt away
As Snowball approaches me
I realise a kitten from Heaven
Has been delivered to me!

Mariam Haidour (11)
Islamia Girls' School

Sandpaper Kisses

Sandpaper kisses
On my hair, cheek or chin
Sandpaper kisses
That's the way for my day to begin
Sandpaper kisses
A cuddle, a purr
My alarm clock is covered with fur!

Hafsah Aaqab (11)
Islamia Girls' School

Twinkling Diamonds

Diamonds twinkling from far away Mars!
Pearls twinkle in my watery eyes
Lights up the ocean as a silver mirror
Diamond is blue as the salty sea
It glows every time I wink at it
It's as white as glacier can be.

Zahra Faiz (11)
Islamia Girls' School

A Difficult Decision

It was with a strange atmosphere that we ate dinner last night,
My parents kept exchanging gleeful glances,
A tingling sensation crept up my spine,
I wondered what was going to happen.

My bursting curiosity was relieved
When my parents, grinning like Cheshire cats
Announced we were moving house,
You could have heard a pin drop.

I was flabbergasted
As the truth slowly sank in, my feelings exploded,
I felt as small as a mouse, as proud as a lion,
So unsure - I just couldn't leave.

Fourteen years I've lived in this house
I know every nook and cranny
Every corner holds a memory
Every wall tells a story.

My house is a box of ancient memories
A basket filled with delightful times
A hamper with sorrowful news
My house was my childhood.

But, let's pause, let's think -
This could be the time for a whole new change
New walls to gather new stories,
New corners to clutch new memories.

What would you say?

Ruba Ramadan (11)
Islamia Girls' School

My Mummy

A person that is sweet
And keeps the house neat

A person that is kind
And she never minds

A person that is happy
As she's changing a nappy

She's always on the phone
And she won't leave it alone

She's the best
In the west,
Because that's my mummy.

Bayan Cevahir (11)
Islamia Girls' School

You Promised

You promised you'd be back for Christmas Day,
The night I caught you sneaking out the back.
You made me promise that I'd never say
I'd seen you with a suitcase and your mac.
So all this time I've kept my mouth shut tight
When mother asked if I knew where you were.
She cries a lot - I cannot stand the sight.
I leave the room, but want to comfort her.
I want to tell her that it's all OK,
That you have just gone temporarily.
And yet I waited, hoping every day
That you'd be back to help put up the tree.
But Boxing Day is here and I can see
That as you waved goodbye, you lied to me.

Sarah Wedmore (15)
James Allen's Girls' School

Mrs C S Lewis

Just imagine a world beyond the wardrobe
He said to me one day
What absolute rubbish can fill a man's brain
At his young and tender age.

'Don't stick your head in there darling.
You know you'll get an awful reaction.'

It seems like we don't talk anymore
Just him and his pen and his big brown wardrobe
That dashes with carpet and marks my beautiful walls.
My beautiful off-white walls.

'Don't bring those moth balls out
And stop tapping on the doors.'

It's absolutely horrifying when he wanders out
Of that awful wardrobe.
With his jacket laden with moth balls
When guests are visiting.

'No you can't bring your supper in there
Just eat it out here.'

Well I guess he might be famous
Because it seems to me
People like idiotic men.

Alison Eson (13)
James Allen's Girls' School

Not A Poet

I am not a poet, believe me
I use poetry to get rid of feelings that won't leave me.
I'm not in love
I need a muse
I can't write everything from nothing like Ted Hughes.
But sometimes in a way
Emotions show you
And sometimes only poetry can say
I love you.
I need to get it off my chest at times
I realise that
It's all for the best
When it rhymes.
And I wonder what do people do
Who have never read Prufrock?
While I watch the world go by in Starbucks
Get a panini
I know I'll never be a genius like Seamus Heaney
But I adore to see the words curl on the page
The world's a stage
And I write my story.

Sophie Renner (15)
James Allen's Girls' School

Short Break

Once, in a land, not long ago,
Lived a toad, a snail, a frog and a crow
From spring till summer they lay on their backs,
Wasting their time like potatoes in sacks.
They bathed in their pond, they sat on the grass,
They wallowed in sunshine, as the months passed.

Summer turned to autumn, leaves brown and old,
Huddled together, toes growing cold.
'I've had enough!' Toad said one day,
'I can't stand this place!' he started to say.
He wanted to leave the frost and the gloom,
And move near the sun, stars and the moon.

'By gum you've got it!' exclaimed the crow,
'Let's pack our bags, where shall we go?'
'To visit my aunt, a cousin or two,
They live under a rock, with a sea view.'
That evening they left, without delay,
On the back of the bird the other three lay.

Comfortable, warm, content and well fed,
Fully prepared for the journey ahead.
They flew for a day and then for a night,
Endured much turbulence throughout the flight.
Soon dark was upon them, thick sheets of black,
Snail grew worried, wanted to go back.

'It's too dark, I can't see a thing!
What if we crash? You may break a wing!'
Still they kept on, under the strain,
Next came the thunder, after the rain.
Not far ahead lay danger unseen,
In the shape of a trunk, branches all green.

Into the tree they flew with a thump!
Frog bashed into toad, her head up his rump.
Necks bent with a crack, arms with a pop,
They dropped one by one, down with a plop.
Squashed like an orange, pulp with the juice
Mashed like potatoes, soft like mousse.

And so the group of unlikely friends,
Painfully met their untimely end
The moral may be, some might say,
Sometimes at home it's better to stay
But if one must fly dark stormy nights,
Attach to your crow a pair of headlights.

Olivia Cerio (15)
James Allen's Girls' School

Untitled

I was often teased for my shape and size
I'm different from them, can't you see?
A man comes to measure me once every week,
But I'm still just as thin as can be.

My friends went away in a great big white van
Each week I am left here alone
The ticket to going away with my friends,
Is not to be just skin and bone.

Mummy and Dad left me sometime back,
As they were a suitable weight,
I wished and I wished I could join them there
As they all drove away through the gate.

It's tedious here without family or friends,
For company I do yearn,
But I know that it's nice where they go - here's how
Though I call them, they never return.

I've often dreamt of the land far away,
But I'm stuck here with tears on my face
I wish I were fatter and chosen to go
To 'Butchers' - oh what a place!

Liz Burgess (15)
James Allen's Girls' School

Mrs Humpty Dumpty

Humpty Dumpty sat on a wall,
My pale, round egg of a husband
Sat on a wall
What an absolute, ridiculous troublesome
First class fool!

'Trust me I'm strong'
'I could easily take him!'
'So what I'm an egg?'
Yes yes Humpty, of course you can do it
Then he'd moan and he'd cry,
How hilariously he would try.

The thing is everybody else knew that he was
                                a fragile & delicate egg.
Everybody else knows eggs don't jump off kitchen work tops.
Everybody else knows eggs don't climb
                onto their wives shoulders and skydive down,
Everybody else knows eggs don't go paint-balling
Or join in with the scrum at rugby.

Poor Humpty just wanted to prove eggs were strong,
Eggs could climb,
And eggs did fight,
But Humpty Dumpty sat on a wall,
And Humpty Dumpty had a great fall.

Eggs don't sit on walls.

It's the law,
Humpty's bottom was as round as a football,
Of course he would fall down,
Silly, silly clown.

Maybe he was just ambitious
I highly doubt that!
Cocky arrogant fool,
Eggs don't sit on walls.

Jess Austin (14)
James Allen's Girls' School

On Meeting A Tiger

A jar of smooth-smooth earth-brown pottery
Upon a little head adorned with strands of night.
A slender frame wrapped in softest, crimson cotton,
Two nut-brown feet with golden rings and soft, soft tread.
But tigers' feet tread softer and human ears don't hear,
The step of velvet pads, oh velvet pads.

Two rivals met at the silver brink, green eyes met,
And green eyes closed in slow admittance.
This is what the human saw:
A noble head, with whiskers fine, a wide, wide mouth
And eyes, oh green, green eyes.

Two rivals met at the silver brink, green eyes met,
And green eyes closed in slow admittance.
This is what the tiger saw:
A tiny cub with coat of red, no stripes,
Two small, small feet and eyes, oh green, green eyes.

On meeting a tiger, one might scream and run but no
The small, small feet stood still and also did
The velvet pads, oh velvet pads.

The tiger dipped its noble head and drank,
Through his wide, wide mouth
His thirst was quenched, and turning,
Walked with swinging stride,
His snake-striped tail all hanging free.

No rustle of burnt-brown leaf or crackling twig,
Disturbed his velvet footed way.
He stalked away on velvet paws,
His red-black back a-curving.

Tiger's feet tread softly and human ears don't hear
The step of velvet pads, oh velvet pads.

Alex Wilson (11)
James Allen's Girls' School

The Limpet Picker

Pre-dawn and she'll be there
Stooped in the darkness,
Picking,
Beneath the looming cliffs
(like she has for the last fifty years)
At the clumsy limpets,
Clinging like children to the rocks.

Her face will be furrowed with annoyance,
At the absence of the agility
Her fingers once possessed,
Gone
Only to be replace by the quivering, inanimate
Old lady's claw.

For her the silence in nature's noise
Gives only a temporary respite,
As the only true player in-between
The unnecessary and inept participation of the chorus,
Who arrive to late to find the essence of the seaside,
Buried beneath the sun, sandcastles and inane chatter of children.

She prefers the crashing of the rocks,
The shattering of the sand,
The crying of the gulls fighting against the wind,
The noiseless grind of fishing boats returning from a night at sea,
And the whispering of the waters,
Hinting at their former lives.

Standing, stooped in the half light of dawn,
Face crumpled by age,
Staring out,
Unconsciously
Shadowed,
By the clasping claw of age.

Cecily Cole (15)
James Allen's Girls' School

Lonely Panda Days

I struggle from sleep to the sound of men
To the sound of a flute and a drum,
But I walk away in fear
These sounds are not for me.
I prefer silence and the deep green of the forest
Slowly waddling through wet leaves.
Dew drips on my nose
It is a pleasure to taste on the tongue -
You do not need to be fast if you are alone.
I do not follow any paths.
There is always bamboo, lazily waving
At the wide and generous sky.
It cracks as I crunch it
The cool juices prick my tongue.
This is the way it has been for all time.
Walking our own way, we always survive.
In the distance, I see human flames
But I turn back as always to the forest again.

Katie George (11)
James Allen's Girls' School

Ego Sum

I am solely, I am
I aim at solid minds of attitude and stealth
Quick to seal and unlock the truth
Turning around the days like they were paper aeroplanes
And slowly pouring out sweet pocketfuls of vengeance unto myself
The feelings reek deeper shades than black and therefore
I accept every broken slash across my arms hoping that I
Will change and become a rock, to hold out and be strong with.
Who is the doctor that will help me out
When I cry and try to block out the stars?
To moan into a silent cave that holds me still
Rocking back and forth my child self in my arms
Receding in that smoke, thinking I will be safe
But I am not, and there is no glory in defeat
And no winning in loss, a great loss that I am
Beginning to shield myself from this storm
Hold me close and beat me unconscious so I might sleep
And be a peace, a liquid form, I fit!
This is the world and this is I,
Dreaming deep the being is,
I am solely, I am.

Kei Lawford (15)
James Allen's Girls' School

Sonnet

Why is it sonnets are all about love?
Is it a sign of a poet's true worth?
Did inspiration come down from above?
Sleeting through Heaven and settling on Earth?
I've never felt such passion or wonder,
Likened a feeling to fresh-blossomed rose.
My heart was never thrown all asunder
By beautiful verse or elegant prose.
We are told love is like light through the dark,
Taste of pure honey, the smell of sweet scent.
The feel of crushed velvet, song of a lark.
Every sense caught, all emotion is spent.
I see that now I have followed the trend
My sonnet too was on love to the end!

Helen Oxenham (16)
James Allen's Girls' School

Africa

Africa, the place I love,
My second home,
I have memories of freedom, family and peace,
Choice, love and hope,
A world where you are treated like a queen,
Where you are valued and important.

But for now I must be here,
To live and love the hard way,
For money, career and competition,
One day I will return,
Like a bird to its nest,
To my one and only home,
Africa.

Annabelle Appiah-Dankwah (15)
La Sainte Union School

Bitter Like The Man Was

If you were to die, how'd you like to be known?
Remembered as the old who's just mean and alone.
He shouts and scares the children senseless.
Really he's just poor and defenceless.
He's grown bitter, cold and bitter,
A bully, his actions show his self-consciousness he's tried to hide
For years with an act of spitefulness and hate.
He sits in that old armchair not moving much,
Everything he needs seems within his clutch.
I always see an evil scowl imprinted upon that old face.
The lines shaped into it, so deep, easy to trace.
Bloodshot eyes, visible capillaries all over the crinkled visage.
That man lives next door, never got over his troubles.
He goes from age to age
Tormented by rage, granted eternal life
We think we're the ones being punished by his presence
But he goes through the decades, and they pass him by
As we do when we die.
Scared me as a kid he did, now I'm bitter for life like him
That's what he wants, so I'm gonna change and won't be known
Like that old guy sitting there mean and alone
Running games still after centuries
But I'll take his advice.
There's one piece I'll accept
'Trust your instinct, stay true to you,
        because of all of us these are very few.'

Katherine Wise (13)
La Sainte Union School

The Silliest Thing

The silliest thing will always be,
Dear piglet swimming in a roaring sea.
He's a scared little fella so of course he would shout,
But it is very silly to go in and about.
Another thing is a circus clown,
Being a yoga instructor floating up and down.
'He looks very funny,' people would say
'Like a human - shaped rainbow flying away.'
The third thing that has come to my mind,
Is a guide dog who is also very blind.
Not chasing cats or helping its patients
But chasing people with nice perfume scents.
I can think of another thing that is incredibly silly.
The statue of Liberty getting married to a Hillbilly.
They would live in a farm, but she'd take most of the space,
And she'd have to eat, maybe the whole entire place.
What else is there? Oh yeah, I remember,
That Earth's best friend is the planet Jupiter,
They aren't close so they'd shout through the stars,
And stars would be speeding as if they were racing cars.
I'm running out of ideas, but there is another,
A princess fell in love with her husband's father,
She forgot her husband would soon be king.
But when the father died, she went to her husband for their ring.
This is the last one I will say,
Whales called dinosaurs to visit and they came that day.
It was a surprise to the people in the city,
'I thought they were in the ground, well that's a pity.'
In my mind these are the silliest things to me
And like I said, they will always be.

Valentina Okolo (11)
La Sainte Union School

The Heart Of Mine

I look out of the window,
See green grass and blueish clouds,
And I think about my most wonderful dream:
If only I could play the piano,
On a warm autumn day!
It was my dream and my imagination,
And it will be forever in me,
Like a little part,
That takes my life from me.
Maybe an hour, maybe two, but
I will sit and listen to the most wonderful composers,
Who were great in their time.
I dream I could have a wonderful voice,
I wish I could sing like the birds in the trees,
With their own beautiful songs.
I wish I could dance, like a butterfly,
From one flower to another,
Or like a Cinderella at the ball.
Music . . .
I am ready to put all my heart in to it,
And play and sing and dance for my own creations.

Liza Turkova (13)
La Sainte Union School

The World

The world is cold and the world is cruel
And they make too many rules.

They lock small creatures up in cages
And banish them to zoos for ages.

But lucky for me I have people to care
Like my mum and dad and my friends who share.

I never thought it would come to this
But I don't feel safe on this planet.

Kasia Giddings (12)
La Sainte Union School

What Is Love?

What is love?
Is it affection?
Is it sex?
Or is it something
That will cause you stress?

Is it learning to trust someone?
Is it learning to know someone?
Is it the truth you are yearning to show?
Or is it the way you are destined to grow?

Love is the feeling that some people hide.
Love is the feeling that spreads worldwide.
Love is the thing some people describe
As the feeling that makes us lose our pride.

Love is something you cannot see,
Love is something that may set you free,
Love is whatever you want it to be,
Love means absolutely nothing to me.

Kemi Odunlami (14)
La Sainte Union School

Beneath

It was beneath the deep waters, where there was
                                    no sight of the coast.
That stillness observed the uprising motion that
                                    carried the sea above.
True anger and hate brought darkness over light,
And though the sun still rose, awakening life,
All beauty was vain and 'belonged to the right'.
The stillness beneath kept a watchful eye,
But like all others, we all must die.
The question is with what reason, with whose power takes the life?
For no one owns what is not in their right.

Mary-Grace Sturley (15)
La Sainte Union School

A Man's Strife

Acceptance sweet acceptance is what I really yearn,
When, oh when will they ever learn?
All alone in my drafty small stable,
I know I'll never be able,
To experience the life of a rich man - stable.

The pain, the anguish I have each day,
Confuses my mind in the strangest way,
I always wish for warm proper bedding,
Instead I receive a box full of hay to rest in.

My crippled back is a limitation to me,
A crippled man I shall always be,
A comforting shoulder - just some company
Feels like somewhat of a necessity.

I can't even play solitaire,
For fear I'll take something from them so dear,
When'll they realise I'm a lonely old man too?
Sometimes I weep when they tell me to 'shoo'
Some of them treat me like I don't exist
Some of them snarl with superior twist.
Oh how I long for my dear father's kiss!
I swear that if he were alive today,
Just for him I will obey,
Yes, indeed every whim I say,
A joyful pair that we will play.

I don't think or talk about my mother as much,
But remember faintly her gentle touch,
Sometimes at night I cry, and cry,
Why did my parents have to die?

Apart from them, some really care,
I depend on them to get by, here and there,
Charity comes but once a week, God in your heart please them keep.

'Lazy' or 'Tramp' they refer to me
Just shows how ignorant they can be,
Nasty words used to separate others,
When deep inside we all are brothers.
The books I read,
Fulfil my need,
They strengthen me before I sleep.

This life is nothing but a tragedy
Oh, why is it such a misery?
I cannot wait till I'm in the sky,
Where up amongst the bright angels I fly,
But for now, I say goodnight.

Sandra Engmann (15)
La Sainte Union School

Love Thee Forever!

Every day and every hour,
When I think, I have the power.
When I'm down and feeling blue,
I'll always, always think of you.
I'll text you, I'll phone you and speak to you,
But remember I'm there for you too!
So don't stop what our love is creating,
You might not know what is waiting.
Keep your friendship, keep your hearts,
Forever together!
I'll love you with all my heart,
So please don't break us apart.

Love thee forever!

Elisabella Cesista (12)
La Sainte Union School

Living In The Big World

Living in the big world
Is no joking matter,
There is lot's to see and remember
So you must learn and at the time also gather!

Here, there are wild animals
Always behind you and stalking,
You'll never know what they might do
As you go out walking.

You see all these busy people around you
You wonder who they are,
Don't forget they're strangers my dear
They could drive you away in their car.

Keep this to mind everyone
Remember it through life,
As you get older to know things better
It'll save you some pain and strife!

Yasmin Osei-Kuffour (11)
La Sainte Union School

Black And White

They are complimentary colours,
Yet the artists do not know,
In this world of black and white,
They are backstage in the show.

Colours help to shape this world,
Red, yellow, green and navy blue
Though these colours have shade and depth
Black and white doesn't come in every hue.

They are simple and unique,
They can't make me feel a special way,
But in this world of black and white
They can still take my breath away.

Stephanie Butler (14)
La Sainte Union School

Dreams

Sitting, chilling, relaxing
Reminiscing about the times I had
Thinking about the good, the bad
The bad times fade away
While the good times shine brighter every day
Thinking about something, nothing
Things which are irrelevant to people who don't care
People who stare and wonder
Asking questions, that have no meaning
Meanings, which are foreign to me
Meanings, which mean nothing to me
Meanings, which I don't search for anymore
Now I'm up here
Flying through space, smelling the sweet essence of Heaven
Heaven, which is so near but so far
So near I can hear the angels playing memorising melodies
But so far I can't feel it against my skin
Now I know dreams can truly come true
Don't let the impossible hold you back.

Jessica Ijoyah (11)
La Sainte Union School

After Winter

After wintertime
The flowers start blooming
Brightly coloured with buzzing bees,
And they have lovely green leaves.
Fluffy yellow chicks
Hatching all day long.
Little baby lambs,
Learning how to run.
The sun is welcomed back.
The sky is summer blue
And everywhere you look,
There's lots of rabbits too.

Louise Hayes (11)
La Sainte Union School

Friends

Friends are there to care and share
They bring happiness into the air.

They bring us up when we feel down
They make your life turn upside down.

They bring happiness to all around,
They are there when we fall down.

They always will be there to care,
To help when no family is near.

When we need help they'll understand
And help by lending a hand.

When there's a battle to face,
They'll be there to tie your shoelace.

They'll always bring a smile to your face,
They'll be there in every place.

If you ever need someone to care
Never trust Bush or Blair.

Always sharing with friends
Helping them to make amends.

Best friends tell each other the truth,
And do not lie or be cruel.

Julia Williams (12)
La Sainte Union School

I Am

I am the locker that holds your secrets,
I am the chair you sit on at school,
I am the key that holds your heart,
I am the pavement that leads your way,
I am the book that holds your work,
Touch me I am nice and gentle,
Feel the softness of my heart.

Lucy Loveder (11)
Notre Dame RC Girls' School

The Ship Of Doom

People crowded like rows of toothpicks
With no air to breathe
No space to see
Air polluted from the smells never imagined
Oh Lord! I need my family
The stench of dirty, stinky people
People who are abnormal to me
Talking abnormal languages
Looking in their abnormal ways
I was a young girl who knew nothing
But feared almost everything
Children falling down a pit of urine
And people dying bit by bit right in my perfect vision
Stayed in my mind and always will
No way of escape
Tied together like wild animals
That are struggling to be set free
Only
Then managed to escape.

Yomi Ogunsola (13)
Notre Dame RC Girls' School

Happiness

Happiness can be great
Happiness can be strong
It is in the darkened sky.
It is in a sunny song,
Happiness is not lucky
Happiness is not dumb
All of this is destined
For those who don't do wrong.

Victoria Olusanya (12)
Notre Dame RC Girls' School

Glow

I feel the rhythm
I feel the drums
I hear the singing
I hear the hums
Around the fire, my creation
Around the fire, the glow
Circling soundly
Circling slow

Pinch of herb
To poison the master
So he won't whip us to make us go faster
So he won't take our women away
And send them crying back with dismay

I feel the rhythm
I feel the drums
I hear the singing
I hear the hums
Around the fire, my creation
Around the fire, the glow
Circling soundly
Circling slow

My creation heats the cauldron
My creation is the light
My creation glows up the nation

They are coming . . .
Die out my glow
Die out my glow

I feel the rhythm
I feel the drums
I hear the singing
I hear the hums
Around the fire, my creation
Around the fire, the glow
Circling soundly
Circling slow.

Jane Jimenez (13)
Notre Dame RC Girls' School

The Serpent Whip

I see it . . .
It wriggles like a serpent . . .
Serpent wriggle round a branch . . .
Waiting to strike . . .

It sees me,
But I run,
I run through thick forest,
Run through the trees,
Not realising its stealth
The smooth and silent slither,
Its yell a hiss,
Its scales turn to cow skin
Preparing to strike . . .

Suddenly I trip,
Too tired and weak to carry on,
No strength to escape,
No will to run,
No future to come,
Only a past to remember,
I brace myself,
And prepare for the shock . . .

I can feel it slithering
I can hear it sing
'There's no way out now,
The time is near,
Brace yourself now I'm here . . .'

I've felt the pain,
I have felt the shock,
And work goes by
Without a stop
But at least I know,
At least I remember
That terrible day
I became their member.

Leanne Gayle & Shelana (13)
Notre Dame RC Girls' School

Power

Ha!
Look at you!
Told ya revenge would be sweet.
Who is in control now you poor fool?
Who now has the whip, which whistles in the air before it strikes?
Who now has the stick whose sole purpose is to break bones?

Who now has the power to haunt you in your sleep?
Who now has the power to bring diseases across your land?
Who now has the power to destroy the crops that bring you money?
Who now has the power to take a knife to your throat?

Who now has the power to make you wake in a sweat?
Who now has the power to cause you to go paranoid and mad?
Who now has the power to take away your life?
To take away your children, the whole family including your wife?

You killed me you stupid fool, you brought this upon yourself,
You've caused me to use my dark magic to return and
deplete your health.
Well now I must go but I'll be back tonight when you sleep,
Oh how I love revenge, revenge is so sweet!

Jasmine Ewhieberere (13)
Notre Dame RC Girls' School

You Are Like Beauty

You are beauty, beauty is you
You are as beautiful as the morning dew.
When I see the sun rising I think of you
If you are not beauty then I wonder who . . .
Your eyes like the stars that twinkle bright
Your skin like silk, your hairs like night
Your innocent face, your tiny feet
You look so harmless, and so sweet
You make even a grown man smile,
You are beauty; you're a newborn child.

Azaria Hastings
Notre Dame RC Girls' School

Half-Caste

Half white
Half black.

Half of him
Half of her.

Half cock
Half hearted.

Half wit
Half smart

Half a slave
Half a master

Half poor
Half rich

Half contaminated
Half pure

Half African
Half European

Half hers
Half his

Half caste
I am half caste.

Geraldine Omofia
Notre Dame RC Girls' School

My Life Is Hard

When I walk through the classroom
And say 'Hello',
No one replies
When I help the person in danger
They don't say 'Thank you'

When they tease me
I tell the teacher,
But they carry on
They think I'm
Invisible.

When I come home
My sister and brother
Bother me
I try to do my homework
But my parents keep
Helping me
When I don't need help.

Then when I go to bed,
I pray.
Then afterwards I say to God:
'Why is my life so hard?'

Beverley Mentoya
Notre Dame RC Girls' School

Lost

M y journey into Hell has commenced
 I am but a mere dime to these people
D oom day has finally come
D oom day has finally come
L ife has come to an end
E verything has been lost.

P ast is my happy life
A nguish controls my new one
S anity has been lost
S anity has been lost
A gony
G rief
E verything is lost forever.

Alexis Okonta (13)
Notre Dame RC Girls' School

School

There was once a school called Notre Dame
It was full of Notre Dame girls.
Year seven girls were wearing light pink shirts,
And very very shiny red bags.
The school is full of happiness
The school is full of joyfulness
The school is never careless.
And we are always helpful
But one thing we all are is a family.

Abiola Danmole
Notre Dame RC Girls' School

My Magic Box

(Based on 'Magic Box' by Kit Wright)

I will put in my box . . .
The tipping sound of a dripping tap.
Candle lights smouldering in the icy winds.
The rainbow-coloured police car racing in the big blue
Sky with white waving clouds.

I will put in my box . . .
The whispering sounds of the whirling winds in the
Scorching Sahara Desert with shooting stars on sandy shores.

I will put in my box . . .
A surfer swimming under the beautiful Bahaman sea.
And a diver riding above the magnificent Malaysian ocean.

I will put in my box . . .
Planets made of bread and cheese with stars made of Milky Bars.
And rocks made of chocolate sponge cake with
rainbow coloured icing.

My box is made of wood and leather with varnished
leopard toes for its hinges.

In my box I shall swoop on ice gliding everywhere.
I will hover up and through the clouds until I fly down and
snuggle up in my bed.

Catherine Achukwu (12)
Notre Dame RC Girls' School

Rising Sun

Deep rustling leaves
A cool blue breeze,
Where the earth meets the sky
In gold, red and green.

I crave the feeling of belonging,
But that has been taking from me,
Ya snide remarks go to me heart
But I have come back for revenge.

Prods in the back,
Whistles in ya ear,
Into your head I'll stare
Your dreams will be mine,
To prod, poke and scare.

Cauldrons bubble happily
Me ringing laugh fills the night
Coming to get you
Coming to get you loud and clear.

'The river like a silky dress'
Smooth and pleasant awaits your death
The time will come Massa when I will not be here,
But then I say neither will you.

Scholastica Akech (13)
Notre Dame RC Girls' School

Our Time Has Come (Freedom)

Rejoice!
Hear my voice,
The bells ring with liberty.
I can hear it cry, 'I'm free',
It's talking to me.

The black man triumphs over all,
No longer will the black man fall.
But white men will answer to the call,
To black masters, they will crawl.

No more crops will attack,
As they're sheaves start fighting back.
'Cause we have the power that you lack,
And we will push you off your track.

Now my story's on its conclusion,
No more beatings and confusion.
My life is no longer a pointless delusion.
As our freedom is now proven.

Now they can't deny the truth,
The constitution is our proof.
As we were their irritating tooth,
Hopefully my life will run smooth.

Judgment Day has finally come,
No more acting or playing dumb.
Now back home to where I'm from,
And this is my final so long.

Shelana Bernadine-Williams (13)
Notre Dame RC Girls' School

'Tis

'Tis a mistake to remember my face
'Tis a sin to forget it

Slithering, coiling, twisting, squeezing.
Every thirsty drop.

'Tis a problem to see my carcass
'Tis an error to bury it.

Reaching, snatching, scratching, touching
Every part of you.

'Tis a strive to slay my brat
'Tis a shot to see me.

Breathless, heartless, skinless, restless
Hunting for my prey.

'Tis a mistake to remember my face
'Tis a sin to forget it.

Marion Osieyo (13)
Notre Dame RC Girls' School

Zebras Of The Desert

Like horses, zebras are very fast
With the sand in their manes.
They race in the desert
Using footprints for their lanes.

Wild and untamed
Sprinting on the dunes
Like mad chickens.
Drinking from an oasis from time to time
Only to realise they've lost the race again.

My dear, look at them go
Like moaning groaners
Black and white stripes in the distance.
As they cry:
'Ha, ha, ha, got you!'

Comfort Nwabia (11)
Notre Dame RC Girls' School

JuJu

JuJu is an art,
The art of which we must start.
This is just the beginning,
This is the beginning of their end.
We have nothing of which to lose,
We have no choices so what do we choose?

Ummm Baa, Ummm Baa,
We call upon the spirits of the other worlds:
Ummm Baa, Ummm Baa
Our blood as common as water,
Our flesh no more than dirt
Sticks, whips and stones hit merely our bones,
We are to them nothing, then how does it hurt?

Hear our cries; hear our moans of pain,
We are now dead in our spirit, in our minds
To see us suffer what do you gain?
We are your chosen ones and we are your children
We call you to help us and give us salvation.

Oluchi Nwandu (13)
Notre Dame RC Girls' School

My Banana

He lies there, snoring in his bowl,
My banana, will he wake up?
He's brown black a true mole,
Crusty, spotty, old.

I pick him up,
He's soft he's tired
I begin to peel his long arms,
His flesh sweet, mushy in my mouth.

The skin, my treasure, a protective velvet coat.

Samuel Nicholson (11)
North Bridge House School

Through A Big Cat's Eyes

Slowly, my eyes open
And I start to rise.
Once again I need
To catch my prey by surprise.
Now I go, hardly awake
To refresh myself down by the lake.
Raring to go I stay low in the grass
Getting ready to run very fast.
I wait and I wait,
Then pounce at a blistering speed.
I'm full of determination
And ache with greed.
I need its flesh upon my teeth
So my cubs won't give me grief.
I jump, soaring in flight
Then the next moment a bloody sight.

Nicholas Rogers (12)
North Bridge House School

The Lion

The jungle is mine.
We know this because I am the king of it.
Trees, leaves, breeze is home.

Wet, cold rain gives a soothing, fresh shower.
The animals; flesh brings good food
To my fangs.

Jungle is bright
Where sunlight streams through.

Jungle is trees, home of green-land.
Big, towering caves are where I sleep
In the darkness.

Jungle is pleasure
Where you like to feast.

Brandon Cassidy (12)
North Bridge House School

Snakes

As I slither along the coarse terrain
I feel my belly scratched:
Sharp stones, twigs and seeds
Piercing my scaly skin.

I have a mushroom-shaped head and beady eyes.
With a flickering tongue I smell my prey's track.
My long sinewy body glides over the ground.
I wear a warning pattern on my back.

My head darting from side to side;
My tongue tasting the dry air.
My eyes fix on a passing lizard
Burrowing in the earth, it's unaware.

My skin brushing blades of grass,
Coiling round the gecko's back.
I crush its bones with ease,
Another successful attack.

Under the rays of the midday sun,
I enjoy my feast my task is done.

Edward Bullock (12)
North Bridge House School

A Friend

A friend is someone we turn to when our spirits need a lift,
A friend is someone we treasure for our friendship is a gift.
A friend is someone who fills our lives with beauty, joy and grace
And makes the whole world we live in a better and happier place.

Anastasia Bakanova (11)
North Bridge House School

My Own Island

It is a boiling afternoon,
The palms of this idyllic isle
Give some breeze for a short while,
The soft lapping sea
Gives peace and solemnity to me.

The shells of the beach
Within my close reach,
This beauty overwhelms me,
What more could I wish for?
The sky is ever-changing, like the
Moods of a wild animal.

Watch the birds bring their food to and fro,
As I absorb suns rays at the
Climax of the day,
Why should I ever flee?
This island is a true home to me.

Everything comes to a standstill as everything
Is in a slumber,
Nature has touched my soul.

Oliver Dyson (13)
North Bridge House School

My School

I remember the desk I used to have in my old school,
The pencils we used to write with are just so cool,
The games we play in PE are the best of all,
When I play football I always trip over the ball,
Everyday the teachers are so helpful, kind and funny,
And my friends buy sweets after school with their pocket money,
My school is just like the second home for me,
But my friend are the most important people to me.

Shi Shi (11)
North Bridge House School

Who Am I?

I am the night's vision,
The guardian of the woodland,
The predator of the night,
The composer of the night-time.
Who am I?

I am wiser than you can ever imagine,
I can see all through my binoculars,
I am the most special finch in the animal kingdom.
Who am I?

I am awake at night,
However, however at night
To when you least conjecture,
I'll give you a fright.
Who am I?

I am an owl!

Allen Grace (12)
North Bridge House School

Town Fox

My vibrant scarlet coat glistens and sparks,
I come awake in the bitter cold dark.
In forests and on streets I silently prowl,
I am still and devious and never do howl.

I creep and crawl and rummage through bins,
I find empty pasta packets and baked bean tins.

I never do emerge in full sunlight,
It's noisy and busy and way too light.

The night is calm, clean and still
Where there are deserted streets and bins to unfill.

Stelio Christodoulou (13)
North Bridge House School

Where Does Chocolate Come From?

Here I am, a wrapper thrown in to the bin, crumpled up and inside out
Unused and unwanted.
I don't like it this way.

There I was on the sweet rack waiting, waiting to be picked up,
But then a hand came upon my wrapper squeezing me unbearably,
None the less I was still bought.
I didn't like it that way.

Or could it be when I was a small cocoa bean
being taken to a factory,
Being crushed and melted and carefully being moved in to my packet.
I didn't like it that way

Or maybe when I was still a cocoa bean,
Nice and cosy in my green pod with my fellow cocoa beans,
Hanging on a little branch just able to hold our weight.
I liked it that way.

Lucas Greenwood (11)
North Bridge House School

Untiring

The pastel colours slice deep into her memory,
Crazy paving gets her thinking.

A broken issue for this fragile frame.
She is harp on the same string,
Three kings won't save her today.

The continuous tumble of soft smoke from her mouth and fingers,
The white ribbons twist her in,
They smudge her visions.

Hands folded over the handle
Of that crumbling leather case,

The bleached lilies still flutter in her flimsy skull,
They have expired.

Wasted on her pastel colours.
Plan your escape route.

Esmé Toler (14)
North Bridge House School

That Teacher

Choked blue eyes throttled and saturated in murder
Past over those petite timid tops, topped with mellifluous strands
Of fearful locks shooting in all sequences,

as they gawked with virtue.
Silence traumatized the entire shaking class.
Then the thunder's merciless cry exploded with fire smouldering,
And hurling crimson sizzling, stormy words,
Refuge was a dream not to be found,
Crushed by the marble spit soaring with these shrieks.
Have I been silenced?
Existing outside, just the contemplation of the head's steps

thumping past me: what will she say if she finds me here?
What will she do?
I want to go!
Help me, please let me go . . .
The narrow hallway growing smaller with the moment

consuming him up;
And his skeletal quaking legs tremble in a

bottomless puddle of yellowness.

David Reuben (16)
North Bridge House School

Fire In Choir

Fire, fire, fire!
And we're in choir,
Everybody is running
And I'm just humming,
Everyone is screaming
And I'm just dreaming,
A boy starts to swear
Whilst I swing on my chair
And let the air blow my hair.

Fire, fire, fire!
The hall is on fire,
I'm only painting
And someone is fainting,
But just in time,
While I was smelling a lime,
We saw the fire brigade
Pour in a blade
Of pure cold water
To not make the room even hotter,
So this was how the fire
Was blown out in choir.

Oskar Piotrowicz (11)
North Bridge House School

Fruit Winder Factory

There I am the fruit in the factory
Slowly being squashed
Limb from limb
Every tiny particle
Every tiny seed
I wait for this pain to end
Waiting for the roller-like machine to finish me
Waiting for this torment to stop
There it is
The final destination
The omega
The end of time
I now see the end of light as I am put into darkness
As I am put closer and closer to my wrapper
I hear more and more children call me 'Fruit Winder'
I struggle and struggle
To try and get out
Then I think to myself
Wait I have no life,
No brain, no soul
I stop immediately
At the Fruit Winder factory.

Daniel McKeever Crowcroft (11)
North Bridge House School

Tropical Paradise

Continuous crowing of the cockerels
Rhythmic reggae over the radio
Shrill shouting from the neighbouring children
Sharp sunshine through the blinds
Another tropical day in paradise.

Roaring buses and hooting cars on bendy roads
Taking colourful people to work and school
'See ya later' and 'hav' 'e good day'
Crowded markets with bargaining buyers
'For you five dollars' and 'incredibly juicy'.

Boats full of freshly caught fish
Entering the village harbour
Trucks loaded with coconuts and bananas
Driven to gigantic cargo ships
En route to an awaiting port.

A blinding sunset ending another hot day
Taking all the stress away.
Time for the bloodsucking mosquitoes
To ruin this part of the day.
Another tropical day has gone away.

Stefan Dockx-Xavier (14)
North Bridge House School

Identity

You say identity is knowing who you are,
But what if you don't?

You say it could be where you are from,
But what if you don't know where you're from?

You say you have an identity,
But how do I know you're not as lost as I am?

You say I should know who I am,
But you don't know that I'm lost in an endless darkness.

You say it could be your dialect,
But what if the words have been scattered through your mind?

You say it could be your culture,
But what to do if that's been distanced from you?

You say it could be the food,
But what if you've forgotten the taste?

But what if you don't know
What your identity is?

What if you were a person who didn't
Have an identity?

What would you do then?

Joshua Ajibade (14)
North Bridge House School

The Bee

A dry summer's day I am there.
I shall greet you sharply
With a vibrant touch.
I shall feel you and hurt you
As I am most feared in the forest.
I shall float freely in the air.

My distinctive sound . . .
You'll hear me coming.
Shriek in fright and squirm;
No harm is meant but I shall hurt,
Nothing heard but my humming.

My wings so frail and shades so bold,
As nature sings to me,
I lap up its sweet juice.
But when my weapon is used,
No chances to grow old.

This weapon is used
In self defence:
An open way to my death.
Unseen, I know not what will happen,
As most feared in the forest,
No more shall I freely float.

Sharim Ponticelli (12)
North Bridge House School

Daniel, My Brother

Young Daniel, he was only 12,
He was given a life with every chance to excel.
In the pouring rain Daniel emerged a bedraggled lad,
Completely shattered, no strength left, a sight so sad.
Escaped seemed impossible, only eternity loomed.
The ever present chasing pack that left him doomed.

The group closing in, impossible to bear,
Was a duplicate of the hounds chasing the hare.
When would it end, he could not imagine, a life free of it,
From whenever he could remember, his appearance was ridiculed.

My name is Daniel Lane, he said in vain,
Not 'Billy Bunter' as he had been called,
Over and over again.

Could not anyone just have been his friend?
One would have done, maybe to help him mend.

It was on Greenmore Street
Where Daniel had said goodbye,
To all his family,
Who will constantly ask why?

Who's to blame for all
The tragedies of this life,
My brother's death,
My sadness and all my strife?

Zoe Sophocles (15)
North Bridge House School

She Was There

The little waves were lapping low
Upon the sunken beach
Hands were reaching from above
But always out of reach.

The fishing boat was weighed too low
As the waves began to rise
All as one they dropped their swords
Rising terror in their eyes.

The ships began to toss and turn
The waves still getting higher
And all at once the storm subsided
Sparing them a gruesome pyre.

They looked around the boats they rode
And saw the seas ablaze
They turned and fled before her wrath
Their senses in a blaze.

They reached a shore of sand and stone
A rounded island with sandy rim
A jungled mountain within unseen
They searched for wreckage till light grew dim.

The little waves were lapping low
Upon the sunken beach
Hands were reaching from above
But always out of reach.

Llewe Gore (15)
North Bridge House School

Puretone

Brillig, Carrol and all alone
And Keats
And the dirt-flecked plastic of the bus stop seats.
But hear that tone
Here in the jungle of dead beats.
The silken ivy is my canopy
Here in the jungle
Where gladiators meet their maker
Put pen to paper
It's safer
What the . . ?
Just listen . . .
Only listen . . .

Awake. Awake! With a start
Oh! Night!
Lord unclasp your oysters, and
Unleash your piercing pearls
Night. Night. Where star-stalkers paw
The ferny floor
And Whaffle-snatters whiffle the air.
Darkness pushes its impalpable body of
Black sinew
Through *my* ivy, past my Candy Kingdom
And into my sun-split eyes.
Up from your stupor, up!
Turn it off.
Mango bombs and CD ROMs
What the . . ?
Just listen . . .
Just listen . . .

Jonathon Birkett (13)
North Bridge House School

She Forest

Far far away jutting out into the atmosphere,
Lies a spirit so evil that even hell spat her out,
A woman with the curse of the banshee.

Her fine grains of sand shimmer,
A mesmerizing sight,
But distant they seem to the forest,
For go deep into the shadows, you will find the demon's lair.

A twisted dray world,
Where Mother Nature is drunk, unnoticed,
And wild braids overpower khaki,
And tribes of savage flowers.

At night the moon draws its white glare,
A shrieking takes place,
And the sky turns a violent purple,
Writhing in its brilliance.

Far off in the specious water,
The white mares rebel against rocks,
They burst in emotional charge,
Like fireworks on a dark sky.

When the sun arises,
The sky shatters, leaving a
Blood-red gash across the blue,
A sight not forgotten.

Beneath the heart of forest,
There she's sprawled, dead to the world,
Only to arise on human superstition,
Where once again she will be, lost to banshee.

Juliet McNelly (13)
North Bridge House School

Who Am I?

I am South African,
I am British,
I was born in London,
I have a British passport,
I have a South African passport,
My parents are South African,
Who am I?

Ek is Suid Afrikaans
Ek is Brits
Ek is in London gebore
Ek het 'n Britse paspoort
Ek het 'n Suid Afrikaanse paspoort
My ouers is Suid Afrikaans
Wie is ek?

I can be who ever I want to be,
I am British today,
I am South African tomorrow,
I'm a Londoner
Who am I?
I am who I want to be
I am who I am!

Ek is wie ek wens
Vandag is ek Brits
More is ek Suid Afrikaans
Ek is 'n Londoner
Wie is ek?
Ek is wie ek wens
Ek is wie ek is!

Sebastian van Zijl (14)
North Bridge House School

Moon My Healing Light

Notional eyes
Daggering down dragooning
From the moon
Knee's yield
Caught in an accelerating tempest
With air stabbing flesh.

Heart pours with envy
Her eyes illuminated with Lobelia
Blossoming into a man's alma
Sizzling, electrifying as sparks
Hold hands like sun and moon.

Why does she poison my
Wound when she knows there's a cut?

Lithe and supple moon is my healing light.

Alexander Robertson (16)
North Bridge House School

The Old Oak Tree

Humans have lived for a long, long time,
Like the old oak tree.
For so many years we have grown and matured.
Like the old oak tree.

All in a variety of shapes and sizes;
Tall ones, short ones, thick ones, small ones,
Old ones, young ones,
Wise ones and the learning.

Some with bark thicker than others,
Some that break and don't repair.
The old oak trees live in woods and forests,
Like us in over populated countries.

Ysobel Dunstan (13)
Queen's Gate School

Deep Inside

Glint,
Shimmer,
Glisten red,
The same knife torn through me.

Used,
Battered,
Forever gone,
The body wrecked by me.

Shattered
Broken,
Deep scarred,
The mind that controls me.

Bruised,
Crippled,
Covered now.
The masked corpse that's me.

Emelia Fiell (14)
Queen's Gate School

Memories

With just one click, your memory is stashed away
Either to your happiness or dismay!
Pictures that represent every day of your life
The pain, the laughter or the strife.
To laugh with others and squeal *'Look at that!'*
'Doesn't my bum look fat!'
Or to remember with a tear-stained face;
The sad points that took happiness's place
Right now; you probably don't care,
But later on, you might want to share
That particular story that the picture represents
Don't use 'I haven't got the time' as your defence
Go get them out! Cherish them more!
Remember it's not in the album but your heart they are stored!
Later on; who knows what had changed!
However the photos and memories remain the same!
Memories stick with us for all our years!
Throughout the laughter, joy and the tears!

Marina Dovey (14)
Queen's Gate School

Man's Best Friend

He sprightly walks down avenues of joy,
And makes me think of me as a boy.

He looks at me and I feel fine,
It makes me glad that he is mine.

When his sweet eyes meet my gaze,
I feel entranced as if in a daze.

All those years I watched him grow,
To be the loving thing I know.

Ears as soft as cotton buds,
I'll cover him in kisses and hugs.

He's always happy to see my face,
Yet never cocky he knows his place.

His hair is golden as the sun,
This bundle of life is so much fun.

I'm sure you're wondering who this is,
It's man's best friend that's who it is.

Joccoaa Hand (13)
Queen's Gate School

Everlasting Time

There is a clock sitting very near
With a tick-tock for me to hear,
It is a strange instrument,
For some it brings hope and joy,
For others it brings fear and lament.
It is always there and it will never stop,
The monotonous sound of that tick-tock.
I nearly fall asleep despite the time,
All because of that repetitive whine.
Time is going to last forever,
No one can destroy it, never, never.
Time is running out and we cannot make it,
So it would be a stupid thing to forsake it.
Time cannot and never will be late,
Just as the hands of a clock are always straight.
Most people find they don't have enough time in life,
So make time for others,
A child, your parents, a friend or your wife.

Amelia Simmons (13)
Queen's Gate School

The Prisoner Of Time

You can see him looking
Through his metal bars,
It's a long time he's been waiting
But no one comes.

He knows everyone here
He's been waiting so long,
He's starting to lose hope here
Looking out singing a song.

He's planning to run away
He can't stand it any longer
But there is something blocking his way
His biggest drawback; fear.

This is hope you can see
And fear is near,
Looking back at me
Whose home is now here.

Leoner du Jeu (13)
Queen's Gate School

Linked Emotion

Love is like an open window,
A blossoming rose.
A special bond,
Beginning with a committed oath.

Fear is like an abandoned street.
Sweaty palms and cold chills.
An instant panic or an instant thrill?

Anger is the smallest spot on your best tie,
A baby shrieking from the start of the flight.
A demonstration,
Of aggravation and frustration.
Anger without release,
Leads to violence, swearing and surreal beliefs.

Love is fear,
Like a branch from a stalk.
But is it love we fear?
Fear and anger are inexplicably linked.
Is love a passion, a sin, or the way we think?

Charlotte Davis (13)
Queen's Gate School

The Tiger Within

Out of my box, burning bright,
Came my tiger dreamed at night,
Crouching down, golden brown,
Came from within me, without a sound,
I met new people and started new lives.
I would feel sorrow, as she would hide,
But growing inside me; burning stronger,
Her time prolonged,
Longer, longer.
They would tell me,
'I want to communicate with you'
I thought there was no point if we didn't need to.
Until yesterday, when I met him,
He was a tiger tamer and he spoke to me,
And let my tiger free,
To live here with me.
Tiger, tiger, golden touched,
Please help me reach the
Places I wish to be.

Stephanie de Giorgio (13)
Queen's Gate School

Jealousy

I feel trapped, unwanted,
With the suddenness of youth I am dismayed.
By my skin, the greenish tinge,
That blackens my thoughts and makes me cringe.

I am crushed by a lie,
That makes me want to die.
I am silent when I feel the pain,
Of a thousand things I want to say.

This layer covering me is poisoned,
I have no thoughts but of what bother me.
But I am never so much in love,
Then when I am covered in the green glove,
Of jealousy for someone else's love.

It sickens my heart,
That wants to tear me apart.
To tell my secret to someone,
To release the burden on my back,
That always weighs two tonnes.

Annabella Tubbs (13)
Queen's Gate School

Rebellion In The Park, One Saturday In July

By the evil of inequality, which is a variant of the whole,
By the infamy of instability, that which lights the soul,
By uneasiness of mind, which is the heart of philosophy,
By injustice apparent, by shadows denied,
The spirit is goaded, and hatred your bride.

Your hands clasped by your side
As you are forced to go with the tide,
The course unnatural, the subjugation of youth,
The epitome of innocence, the death of your truth,
And your tears are blackened by thc fire of your eyes.

A mess of word pinning your heart to the depths of your soul,
Poison seeping through the seams of your teeth,
But they can't tell, no, though you wish them in hell,
For what are you if you feel nothing
But an empty, black pit yourself corrupting.

Rage stands on the shoulders of your fears,
Shut it out, close it, blank it with tears,
The rage subsides, but can your angry heart deny
The painted wiles that did supply
Yourself with an all-consuming smile?

Meredith Winter Kerr (13)
Queen's Gate School

Shadow

I turned away it seemed to grow,
And reminded me of a familiar foe.
Like looking into a mirror, it haunted me,
Looming shadows, growing like seed to tree.
Out of sight but always there -
Mocking, playing games it began to tear -
Devouring, preying on my mind
Deceiving madness made me blind.
Like a withered rose, dead and black.
A shadow, menacing, staring back
I dared not look at what others saw,
A nightmare turned into something more,
Pretending something real was not true,
The shadow blinding my senses grew and grew
Reflection distorted in the mirror,
Face faded like an old picture.
Locked away in a room with no door,
With only darkness as a friend, it left me raw,
Taken apart piece by piece,
Courage relit the flame of belief.
I looked one day that fateful day, came face to face,
To find nothing more than nothing in its place.

Vicky Lim (13)
Queen's Gate School

The Prison Sentence Of A Wooden Bird

'I can see people
Happy laughing. There are cars, flashing lights, and children
Perfect view. Pity it's been sliced down the middle
Eight bars to chop it into segments and
Remind me who I am, what I did
I eat, I sleep, I drink, I stare, I dream! . . .'

'I am a cuckoo clock. I come out,
Every hour on the hour
I try to settle in the world around me,
Succeed in catching everyone's attention for a moment,
Then I am wrenched back, cruelly flung into darkness
No one cares what I do once I'm locked inside.'

'At least you can scream,
I am mechanical; I have no emotions
That's what people think
But my life is an hourly indecision of forwards
And backwards. Just as yours is pacing round the room.'

'I forget my human nature with no one to talk to.
I can be still and silent for hours at a time.'

'Both of us are functioning machines
Misunderstood, shunned by humans,
We live and wait for death.'

Rozalind Stone (13)
Queen's Gate School

Box

When I saw it sitting there,
I didn't mind, I didn't care
Whether it was there or not,
I didn't care, no, not a lot.

But suddenly, the thought came to me
Why is it there? And I began to see
That the box was not boring at all,
It drew me towards it; it began to call.

It could be empty with nothing to hide,
Or hidden deep down, deep down inside
Could be a present that brings happiness and love,
Better than a rose, or a white, white dove.

For someone the box could be a home
Or moving house, or just being alone
By yourself in your own special place,
You never know, that could be the case.

The box could mean harvest; the box could mean joy,
The box could mean giving a gift or a toy.
To someone less fortunate than yourself,
Instead of it just gathering dust on a shelf.

So, something as simple as a cardboard cube,
Could be so much fun, and could even prove
That you should not judge a book by its cover,
Not just with a book, but with one another.

Lydia Jones (13)
Queen's Gate School

Desolation

Desolation is drops of dreary rain,
Diagonally slashing against the windowpane
The windows rattle harshly -
From the fierce blowing wind,
And misery like a grey cloud
Hangs over your bowed head.

The raindrops so strong,
Keep you locked inside your house -
Like a prisoner behind bars.
There's sorrow as you look out of the shaking windows.
Hail starts to come down.
It pounds, then bounces off of the hard pavement.
You're stuck inside,
Nothing to do, nowhere to go.

Rain comes down faster and faster
Drops trickle down the window –
Like tears rolling down a cheek.
Sighing, your cold breath makes mist on the glass,
Where a white, frosty patch is now present.
Suddenly the rain turns to light drizzle.
A ray of glowing light appears –
Through the sultry clouds.
The rain has come to a halt.

Bright colours appear in streaks across the clear sky.
Hope has come at last.
It lifts your spirits,
And the frown turns to a gleaming smile and a glowing face.
The rainbow has shone through the rain.

Anne Uva (14)
Queen's Gate School

The Seer Of All

Look through and see life
Emotions rolled into one
Contained is deep love and beauty,
Great friendship, hope and help.

Locked away is greed and hatred
Evil and jealousy are there too
They share the smallest of spaces
So when they can, they take charge.

When they see something they want
They push the others out
All is forgotten about deep love,
Hope and beauty. This magical object.

Is used unfairly and hurtfully
We could stop it if we wanted to
But nobody does, they just stand
And watch their body taken over.

They show us everything
After taking it in themselves
We can replay anything we want
With just our magical minds.

They can ward off evil
And even control our fate
They are what give us colour
And beautiful, brilliant eyes.

Aislinn Kane (13)
Queen's Gate School

Grief

When I think of you, I think of the
Wonderful times we had together,
Those magical trips to the park and the beach,
I wish it had lasted forever.

When I think of you, I think of the
First time I ever met you;
The first day of school I had no one to talk to,
But you sat with me, like a friend would do.

When I think of you, I think of the
Trouble we both ran into;
It makes me smile to think that you and me
Wrecked so much! I hope you thought so too.

When I think of you, I think of all the
Times the two of us cried;
Whether it was mourning or fighting. It doesn't matter,
My sadness I could not hide.

When I think of you, I think of the
Promises we made;
To never spoil our love and friendship,
To never let it fade.

Now I look back and see how happy
You have made me. I stand by your tombstone and
It saddens me to think that now,
I am alone.

Claudia Fragoso (13)
Queen's Gate School

Hunger

The lunch bowl sat empty and lifeless beside me,
My stomach was pleading for food,
But once again, the devil deprived me,
Of taking a mouthful of soup.

I felt weak to the bone,
I didn't feel real,
I wanted to groan and groan.

How could this be,
This was calamity,
I needed to eat,
I wanted to eat,
I had to eat!

The town has been bombed two days ago,
All the food was lying in front of me as ash,
The place looked deserted and cruel.
All because of some fuel.

I had made a dash,
Before the crash,
But I knew no one else had,
All of this was making me mad!

Was I alive or was I dead?
It didn't make a difference in my head,
I was in pain,
And the strain,
Was causing me not to care.

'That's it', I thought,
I'm going to die,
But before I do,
Let me ask,
What did I do to deserve this?

Francis Montgomery (13)
Queen's Gate School

The World In A Box

This box is full of mystery,
A container of secrets untold.
It may bring stories from the future
Or maybe some of old.

A bundle of emotions, contained in one small place,
But with the knowledge and wisdom of the whole of outer space.

It's been around since the beginning of time,
And will be there till the end
To save maney hopeful minds
And straighten those made to bend.

So open it up,
To view this place
From someone else's point of view,
But keep it quiet then shut it tight,
'Til this perfect world comes true.

Daisy Armitage (13)
Queen's Gate School

Mum's The Word

When you fall over,
Mum's the word.

When you're hungry and want feeding,
Mum's the word.

When we're brought into this world
Mum's the word (again).

All of your life you have taken this word
For granted and
It's used instead of 'Can I have . . ?'

Just remember who loves you
More than their own life:

Mum's the word.

Frankie Knight (11)
St Joseph's Academy for Boys, Blackheath

Night Ride

When I can't sleep
I shut my door
And sit on the rug
On my bedroom floor.

I open the window
I close my eyes
And say the magic words
Till my carpet flies.

Zooming over gardens
Chasing after bats
Hooting like an owl
And frightening the cats.

Then when I feel sleepy
And dreams are in my head
I fly back through my window
And snuggle down in bed.

Joshua Ayodele (11)
St Joseph's Academy for Boys, Blackheath

A Scary Monster

It started when I went inside the garage.
I saw a big thing, tall, red eyes.
Big, sharp teeth.
The dragon tried to fire flame at me,
It came at me, but
I moved out of the way.
Running from the dragon . . .
Safe.
Home.
The dragon was not there.

Okeima Scarlett (11)
St Joseph's Academy for Boys, Blackheath

Fear

It is always around you
You can feel it, but you cannot
Touch it.
You cannot hear it, but you can
Sense it.

Horror can make you jump,
But cannot make you cry,
It will certainly give you goosebumps,
And I was asking myself why.

Horror is very scary,
But it is what people want to see,
Horror is based on fear,
It is all you can hear.

Maybe people like scary sensations.
For me it will always stay frightening -
But I know that the fear isn't real.

Killian Negros (14)
St Joseph's Academy for Boys, Blackheath

Horror Poem

In the night-time darkness
In the night-time cold,
Did you spot a Catherine wheel
Raining showers of gold?
Did you watch a rocket
Go zoom into the sky?
And hear a bonfire crackle
As the sparks lit up the sky?
In the night-time darkness
In the night-time cold,
Did you clutch a sparkler
As it scattered stars of gold?

Matthew Ayodele (13)
St Joseph's Academy for Boys, Blackheath

Science

Science is imagination
Imagination is you
Seems to be quite complicated
Yet very true.

Science is the greatest romance
A scientist could ever feel
Hug the sun and
Kiss the moon
And to sit back and chill.

Science is magic
Feast your eyes on wonders
Unknown to man
Greatest secrets to be plundered.

Science is a feast of knowledge
Bring your hunger of interest
Feed your mind with the greatest delights
Science is there for you to caress.

Science is imagination
Imagination is you
Seems to be complicated
Yet very true.

Baribor Giokabari (11)
St Joseph's Academy for Boys, Blackheath

Great Minds

Great minds are special
Great minds are unique
Great minds can be quite modern
Or very old and antique.

Great minds are Einstein's
Great minds are Shakespeare's
Great minds are Usher's
That make us all go yeah!

Great minds are always perfect
Never a foot out of place
They have to have the perfect smile
And a glamorous looking face.

Great minds are successful
Some are known worldwide
While others nearly getting there
With only hope by their side.

Samira Ahmed (13)
Skinners' Company School (Upper)

Oprah Winfrey

Oprah Winfrey?
Isn't she so unique
If it wasn't for her
Who knows, people would still have problems
Nobody knew she would make it through.

Oh! She is intelligent
Sweeping the courtyards of her house
One day she helped someone who was in pain
The next day she was helping millions of people.

She is so gifted and talented
Clever and wise
Rich up to this moment
Oh! How I knew Oprah Winfrey would rise!

Debbie Shobo (13)
Skinners' Company School (Upper)

Survival Of The Clever One!

I am being bullied because I'm clever
Leave me alone they never,
What a great gift, the great mind,
You'll be amazed what you can find.

I'm very unique so they say,
Thinking about school I lay,
Quick, smart, super
Still they call me a loser.

Run home feeling upset
Brother calling me teacher's pet
Teachers calling me brilliant
Shouting and yelling *'stupid infant'*.

A genius just like Einstein
Like a light I shine
Like a running tap my tears leak
Everyone just calling me a stupid geek.

Great minds think alike
I hate the big fat bully Mike
Successful I wish to be in my career
Bullies is the thing I fear.

If you let them in
But they won't ever win
If you cling to your pride
And just push them aside
And eventually you will be proud.

Khaleda Begum (13)
Skinners' Company School (Upper)

Great Minds!

One day I got smart
I was happy to succeed
Then struggles came and names were being made
This was where my intelligence was leading
Days past and past
I grew smarter and smarter
This is the way I'm meant to be
But my classmates said no
And wouldn't listen.
Saying you can't be smart naturally
So on my way home I'd turn a corner
They would give me a special beating
They'd say start acting stupid
I want a good mark too.
They'd kick me and leave me hurting
So from that day on I'd save my smartness
Being smart that wasn't me
Including in tests I'd go slow not fast writing
As many wrong answers as I could see
So if you are smart don't let it go
I just didn't want to get bruised
But try your best all you can
Though try not to get accused.

Karess Laidley (12)
Skinners' Company School (Upper)

Great Minds

They say a great mind is smart
They say a great mind is unique
But I know a person that's more than that
And it stays in my heart.

The smartest person I know is my dad indeed
The way he works things out quick within speed

My dad is gifted with a large brain
It's too big to be contained
He's as wise as a monk; he's an extraordinary person.

He can never hide his intelligence
I wonder how he got that smart
Is he an alien, out of this world?

He's as smart as Einstein; he's as smart as a mind wizard
So clever to create a blizzard.

A great mind would be smart
A great mind is where I start
Great minds are you and me
A great mind is my dad
Me too!

Taimmy Asino Iyaloo Hango (14)
Skinners' Company School (Upper)

Great Minds

Genius People

People who have heads
People who have minds
They are always worthy
Always kind.

Teacher asks a question
They put their hand up
Everyone gets jealous
So they say 'shut up!'

Every answer right
Every writing tight
They are always the best
So they can pass the test.

Genius are bright
So they have to
Get everything right.

Sara Lumona (12)
Skinners' Company School (Upper)

What About Me?

I wish I had an opinion,
Just like everyone else.
I wish I had an opinion,
One that made sense.

I wish I had a say in things,
So people won't mess me around.
I wish people would listen,
Once in a while.

I wish they would all be dumb,
Then I'll get all their marks
I wish I could be Shakespeare,
Then everyone would look up to me.

The teachers just keep rubbing it in,
She's not good she needs to read.
Don't they ever think of what I want?
Don't I exist?
What about me?

Angela Paul-Gomez (12)
Skinners' Company School (Upper)

My Cousin

My cousin he's so young
But has a great mind
He's as sneaky as a mouse,
My lovely cousin.

He knows everything
Especially about WWE (Wrestling)
He's so smart; he knows when to do his homework
My lovely cousin.

He acts like a baby
But knows things, mostly everything
He's even smarter than my 9-year-old brother,
My lovely cousin.

But guess what he's only . . .
7 years old and very clever
My wonderful cousin.

Esther Adewusi (13)
Skinners' Company School (Upper)

My Sister Has A Great Mind

I just couldn't understand her,
She's like a postponeless creature,
When she's set to do something,
You just can't stop her,
I always thought she was weird
I don't know why I don't understand her.

She was always praised by the family,
Here and there, she's glorious
She always tried to make me perfect,
She was so annoying,
I thought she was weird,
I don't know why I didn't understand her.

I loved her so much
She annoys me so much,
When she's gone, I missed her so,
I always thought, she was weird.
I didn't know why I didn't understand her.

Zainab Momoh (13)
Skinners' Company School (Upper)

My Sister Sonia

My sister Sonia has a great mind,
She is clever and unique,
And smart and kind,
She's strong and bright and isn't at all weak!

My sister Sonia is gifted,
She's wise and thoughtful,
She's very talented,
One day I know she'll be very successful.

My sister Sonia is very loving,
Happy, cheerful and caring
She's always looking out for me,
And we're never fighting and swearing.

My sister Sonia is very special
She's definitely one of a kind,
She's got a beautiful smile,
And also a great mind!

Ayesha Ahmed (14)
Skinners' Company School (Upper)

My Mum Always Says

My mum always says
'Great minds think alike'.
I didn't believe her
But that was then.

It's always the same,
I think that I've come up with something,
But I found out that someone else was first
Like Einstein or someone.

My mum always says
'There's an artist in everyone'.
I didn't believe her,
But that was then.

It's always the same,
I think I've drawn the greatest,
Then I found out that someone's drawn better
Like Picasso or someone.

My mum always says
'Some people are smarter than others'
I know that's true,
Because she's the smartest person I know.

Subhadra Greco (13)
Skinners' Company School (Upper)

I Am Not Yet Born

(Based on 'Prayer Before Birth' by Louis MacNeice)

I am not yet born; O hear me.
Let not the stuff and fluff, the filth and stealth of tabloid terrors
And all their errors come near me.

I am not yet born; console me.
I fear the world will flood and freeze me,
Scorch and torch me, shake and take me,
Blow and bleed me, lure and lead me.

I am not yet born; provide me
With food to feed me, seas to sooth me,
Nature to nurture me, kin to be kind to me
Friends to find me, health and healing,
Happy feeling.

I am not yet born; forgive me.
For the sins I will commit, the lies
I will live, the tales I will tell, the layers
Of laziness that cover me well, jealousy's
Felony, rage and wrath, the fires of desire,
Never giving enough.

I am not yet born; create for me
A home to be happy in, love that won't leave,
Stars to steer by and a world filled with peace.

Caroline Gillies (14)
The Children's Hospital School

The Conversation

Their conversation was quite unique,
For it took place up in the sky.
An interesting conversation it must have been,
Between two dear old friends.
Both clad in grey overcoats,
And a bowler hat on top.
One possessed a stick,
For he had a limp.

They stood there for hours,
And hours upon end,
Never stirring from their spot.
One day they decided to walk,
To walk as far as they could.
So off they walked into the distance,
The man with the limp,
Limping behind.

They walked and walked
'til they could be seen no more
As they walked right off the picture.

Sergei Palmer (13)
University College School

St Michael And The Devil

There St Michael triumphantly stands,
After having defeated the Devil,
The look on Michael's face is of bravery and courage
And the look on the Devil's is of fear.

The Devil, such an indescribable creature
Looking up at his victorious enemy.
The donor Juan prays untroubled
Right in front of the unholy Devil.

Krish Vaswani (13)
University College School

Ophelia

O' look at my love,
She is sunken yet still above,
The water that hath encased her mind,
Her body, her soul!

O' how I remember the days
When we danced so jolly and gay
But those days are done and over
Because I live on and you live no more.

O' since your death my life's been a shambles
It's been like rolling in a field full of brambles
But now I have the answer.
The answer to all my pain.

O' my dear Ophelia I can go no more
I need you beside me to guide me home once more
With this dagger I shall take my life,
For living holds no pleasure without you my dear wife!

Ben Charles-Williams (13)
University College School

Water Lily Pond

The sunlight glittered on the water
The willow drowns its lower leaves,
The old bridge sways from side to side, creaking ominously
The water lilies, like little children's hands
The mist like thousands of shimmering silver souls
No one knew what could be hidden in the willow's dangling strands,
Or how old the bridge was
Had it stood there since the beginning of time,
Spanning the seasons, immovable?

Max Hofmann (13)
University College School

The Companions Of Fear

There they stood,
As sentinels on watch,
Underneath the dark black hood,
The cold, not just a touch.

Companions of fear,
They stood by each other,
Not one tear,
Was shed for a lover.

The night grew on,
Older and older
The further it went
Colder and colder
A ray of hope
Touched the edge
Thus it finished
They flew from the ledge.

Max Bushman (13)
University College School

The Chair

It sits, in the middle of the room
Still in the cold and damp
It waits and waits for its seat to fill
Uncared for
Unused
Fragile legs
Its frame wrecked
Some bits are missing
Feeling quite vexed
Will somebody please sit
In this old wooden chair
All on its own
It needs somebody to be there.

Theo Weiss (14)
University College School

Good And Evil

Who will fail? Good or evil, right or wrong?
The victors always lift their bleary eyes,
As the end of the day, the fight's been won,
The good turn their tired heads to the skies.

Good beating evil is a worn cliché,
Which time has made into a common theme.
As sure as the sun will rise the next day,
The good will rise above the losing team.

The youthful hero is a famous role,
Which no 'good' tale should ever be without.
'Carpe diem' as he attains his goal,
Should his success be sure? With a doubt.

Contrary to what some people may say
Few tales end with evil seizing the day.

Andrew Mobbs (13)
University College School

Portrait Of A Lady In Red

These cities of slaves where slaves walk free
And yet live under tyranny
Of masters who steal their money, steal their minds
These are the slaves of modern times
And half a world away, there are others
Children parted from their mothers
Who toil all day, work all night
And don't resist for fear of fight
For what they make they're pennies paid
But it's sold for hundreds - such is trade
Bought by the slaves of our first verse
Who buy in earnest, who empty their purse
Who cannot see that what they do is vile
These slaves are prisoners of style

Sam Kriss (14)
University College School

The Scream (1893) – Edvard Munch

I walked carefully watching every step of mine,
I looked ahead and saw my line
The bridge was there waiting,
I stood while my body and brain were debating,
Should I stay, or should I go?

No one has the right to judge me on my looks
Everyone treats me like a pile of unread books,
I never got the chance to prove myself as a human being
People just assume a monster is what they're seeing,
Should I stay, or should I go?

Now the time had come,
I can't say goodbye to my adopted son
In my heart I was always dead
Now it's time for me to bow my head.
Should I stay? No, I think I'll go.

Eliot Tang (13)
University College School

The Mona Lisa Smile

There she is just sitting there. Outside looking calm,
Inside though screaming perhaps and even sweaty palms.
She has a certain smile, cheeky, sickly no one knows,
Her eyes look very gentle and sweet although that all goes,
Once you look at the bigger picture it seems that she is scared
Maybe even petrified perhaps she does not even care!

After all she hasn't got much of a body or a face
So why would she want to be painted in portrait and grace?
The clothes she wears are dull maybe to match her hair,
My guess is she wanted people to look, think and stare.
Her smile could of course just be innocent to make us ponder.
I don't believe it. How about you? Well I guess we'll always wonder!

James Emanuel (13)
University College School

The Scream

A distant howl, a deafening shriek is heard across the sea,
The winds across the sea harbour make you feel free,
From the bridge you can see the beautiful sunset,
It makes you feel that the whole view is just one big concept.

People pass it every day and don't seem to make a scene,
But every day, it's standing there and giving out its scream.
It laughs, it cries, it frowns, there's no ending to it all,
Sometimes it makes you feel so small and sometimes so tall.

It doesn't seem to move from its place on this piece of wood,
One noise from this creature can change your entire mood.
Everything seems to hear its cries, from the sky down to the sand.
I'm sure many people much rather hear a marching band.

It's suffering and dying, every day out on its own,
But no one seems to really care all they do is groan.
It's so depressed and miserable, all it does is howl and scream,
One day its wish is to be realised, that's its perfect dream.

Roie Spitzer (14)
University College School

St Michael And The Devil

St Michael was an angel of red and gold,
One would stop in awe to watch his wings unfold,
Then freeze as he draws his mighty blade,
Making even the Devil look afraid,
With armour glinting in the sun
He bores down on the Devil like hounds on a fox
                                    when hunting has begun.
And soon St Michael deals his final blow
And leaves behind his defeated foe.

Edmund Roberts (14)
University College School

The Scream

As the scream stands still his cry travels miles
Across the ocean and out of the Earths tiles,
Not a response or a sign to help him cope,
But a friend from up above to give him some hope.

To let out all his anger he opens his mouth wide,
And his face goes pale as if he has just died,
He says what he wants to as no one really cares.
Except his only friend, only gift from his prayers.

As the scream stands still his cry travels miles,
Across the ocean and out of the Earths tiles.
He's on the verge of losing it and letting his life go,
But first must figure out who's this friend that says 'no.'

Could it be an angel or could it be a devil?
Could it be a saint or could it be a rebel?
Suddenly he stops and no one makes a sound,
The wind stops blowing and the Earth stops spinning round.

He now knows his friend and will never let him go,
This friend lies within himself and in a mirror he will show . . .

Joel Suissa (14)
University College School

The Scream

Look at his face, white in fear
Look how his hands, clasp his ears
Look at his eyes, so big and bright,
Look how they shine, so fiercely white.

And there he screams on the banister top
In front of the sky, burning so hot.
And with his mouth opened so wide,
Just how many feelings can he hide?

Karandeep Sawhney (13)
University College School

The Floating Conversation

(Based on the art work called 'The Act of Conversation')

'Hello! How do you do?'
'Hi! I'm fine thanks, and you?'
'Well it is a nice day,
Then I must be fine, I'll be on my way.'
'Wait! Please don't go
I've got two cups of tea on down below.'
'I would rather like to come
If you could connect the ground with my bum.'
'Yes, I know how you do feel
I can't stand, sit, not even kneel!'
'Well, we will have to be bold
Otherwise our tea will get cold.'
'You go first and I shall follow
Go and jump right down below.'
'Are you joking, are you mad?
That's the most insane idea you ever had.'
'I shall tell you what we'll do
Not by one, we'll go as two.'
'Fine! I am obliged to agree
As my buds are craving for that tea.'

Buying!

'Oh dear, what a sham
That didn't quite go to plan.'
'No, I didn't think so,
How about another go?'

Saul Goldblatt (14)
University College School

Unrequited Love

A woman had a baby by the sea,
But she was too protective which was a horrendous tragedy.

She loved her son so much,
But he couldn't feel her warm and gentle touch,
She sometimes treated him so unwell,
That his heart level often fell,
One day a serious incident occurred.
That made the whole relationship quickly stir,
One day it got out of hand,
Because of the son's selfish demand,
The mother tried her very best to keep him pleased,
The son though acted as struck by the needing disease.

They fought and fought,
But never seemed to think,
What would she do without him?
What would he do without her love?
One day the son left her,
Without saying a goodbye,
Once the mother found that her precious son had left,
She ran to the closest pier and screamed because she was petrified,
One day when she could take it no more
She jumped off the pier in sight of her returning son's greedy eyes
He went back home and took the house,
It was his entire eager plot.

Christopher Harvey (13)
University College School

Lady In Red

O'lady in red
How I wish you
Were not dead
I want to kiss you,
Because I dearly miss you.

When you were living
You were giving,
But now you're dead,
My heart's like lead.

There once was a veil,
Upon your head
But now that veil's like you,
Dead.

I saw you were ugly, when
I took you in
While I was drinking my
Best gin.

The assassin hath killed
You,
He was going to
Shoot you
But he stabbed you in the back
After you took off your rucksack.

Andrew Pym (13)
University College School

The Battle Of San Romano

The king brandished his shining armour
His troops, his army began to stare
He waited for the signal
It came a minute later
Battle cries roared from the woods
A blur of grey came rushing out
The king was taken by surprise
His eyes showed no emotion
He cries a word
Inaudible it was
His men charged forward
The sound of battle rose into the air
Unfortunate men running to their doom
The sound of the poor and dying
The screams of the wounded
Pierced the atmosphere
The enemy came rushing forward
Trampling those which were in the way
An arrow swished through the sky
Piercing an unfortunate horse's neck
The king sat there
Tears on his cheeks
A few words escaped his pursed mouth
'Was it worth it!
The crown, the horse, the king, the men?'
A javelin pierced the dying king's heart
The king already wounded
He lay there on the bloodstained ground
His fate sealed by war.

Alex Yepifanov (13)
University College School

Vincent's Chair

(Inspired by Van Gogh's painting 'Chair')

So inviting yet much unwelcoming
So lonely yet much popular.

Your contrast surprises me;
The red floor you sit on
To the blonde wooden bones you are made of,
The white wall that is your background
To the green that is your door.

Nothing seems to mix
Nothing seems to go,
But I can tell the colours were meant to be
Because one thing goes
The box in the corner
Brandishing Vincent's name.

The things that lie on your body;
A wrapped tight tobacco
Sitting within a tattered paper
Next to a pipe,
Chair - has your owner left?
Yet is he coming?
Is Vincent your creator?

Are these his favourite things?
Or is he welcoming me to sit on; your tight straw chest,
To pick his pipe, relax and smoke

Looks so comforting yet much forbidding,
So inviting yet much unwelcoming
So lonely yet much popular,
Contrasts of Vincent's chair.

Edward Alexson (13)
University College School

The Scream

I was walking along the bridge on my way to a hospital appointment
I was late and blood-red streaked the sky.
Suddenly, I saw myself, as a child on that bridge,
                              playing with my brother
It was night, we were forbidden to be out of the house
We would come here secretly at the weekend.
That was when we saw them, two men under the bridge,
                    dumping a large bag into the murky bottomless sea.
My brother, unaware, of what was happening,
                              walked towards me.
I couldn't stop him.
A loose board creaked, they had heard him.
They were afraid and vaulted onto the bridge
Within seconds they had grabbed my brother from behind.
I was paralysed with fear; pressure was building in my head.
They struggled; a knife was plunged into his heart
His howl seemed to go on forever as blood rushed from the wound
The planks of the bridge were stained with a trail of rusty red,
                              pouring like a never-ending ribbon.
I felt unsteady as the horror struck me.
I was caught in a nightmare
I ran, and ran,
But am forever haunted by the scream.

Eden Dwek (13)
University College School

Changes

C olourful butterflies fly through the air
H oney apples drop down trees, down, down, down.
A nd there was the gate, shaped as a pear
N ow colourless butterflies dying on the floor.
G orgeous apples are no more
E verything is dead, colourless and bare
S omething has happened over here.

Kathleen Cabigas (12)
Ursuline High School

Not The Next Victim

They drove by slowly . . .
Wound down the tinted windows,
3 . . . 2 . . . 1 . . .
Bang! Shot! Screams!

What business of mine
As long as I'm not
The next victim.

People crying standing
Around her. Danniella
Lying in a puddle of red blood,
Helplessly, suffering and in pain.

What business of mine
As long as I'm not
The next victim.

Why did they do it?
She was a bubbly girl,
Coming from a funfair with friends.
Why? I can't answer the question.

What business of mine
As long as I'm not
The next victim.

Mourning for Danniella
Who is our hearts,
Hoping to find her selfish killers.

What business of mine
As long as I'm not
The next victim.

Bang!

Paige Rippon (12)
Ursuline High School

May The Weather Be Good For Ever.

May the blessings of the weather always shower,
And shed their sweetness on the air for ever and ever.

I like the sun when it shines upon you,
And warms your heart for it to glow.
Its friendly greetings sprinkle light,
In your eyes so its love can show.

I like the rain when it's soft and sweet,
When it washes your spirit fair and clean.
It always knows when to fall,
Softening the soil as it's always been.

I like the soft and crystal snow,
When it lightly lands in heaps everywhere.
It touches and cools me deep within,
And sparkles bright with love and care.

But I hate the cold and stormy weather,
When the hailstones break my bones away.
When the lightning strikes from tree to tree,
And growls to ruin a lovely day.

I hate the cold and frosty wind,
When the hurricanes wildly steal our homes.
I hate it when it howls like mad,
In Florida now, like a ghost it roams.

I hate the monsoon in India,
When the water drowns us to the top.
It batters things down like dirty dough,
And also destroys the farmers' crop.

I hope the weather is always good,
But let's all enjoy it while we can.
'Cos the bad weather comes so soon,
It blows the good ones like a fan.

Aamina Qazi (12)
Ursuline High School

Listen Mr Bus Driver

Listen Mr bus driver,
Who drives like sloth,
As de school bell approach.

Listen Mr bus driver
Whose pace gathers speed,
As me poor old gran
Gropes for a seat. Who jostles and bustles
As mums carry babes
And thump out the beat as if in a rave.

Listen Mr bus driver
Who never has change,
And leave me standing
In de pouring rain
Or finds it funny when I'm wet to de bone
Coz your wheels through de puddle
Created mini tidal wave.

Listen Mr bus driver,
Stop being a pain!

Fisayo Fadahunsi (11)
Ursuline High School

Home

A home? I need one . . .
The wind is cold
The streets are rough
Where should I stay?

Droplets of rain are falling
My soul is burning
No home to live in
A door to stay in

A home is what I need
A place where I can read
A home at last.

Anne Felice Soria
Ursuline High School

Life's First Ten Years

These first ten years,
The most important of all.
But if you're old, and can't remember.
Here's my summary for y'all.

The first and the second,
You don't really know,
The third and the fourth
You're continuing to grow.

The fifth and the sixth
You're striving to learn,
The seventh and the eighth
You've got energy to burn.

The ninth and the tenth
Are simply the best
'Cause you're growing up
Just like the best.

Alia-Michelle Supron (13)
Ursuline High School

Sleeping Rough

Sleeping on the floors at night
Cold and lonely out of sight
On the hard floors I lay till the night-time turns to day.
Then on my feet as I walk through the town
Tapping all the way there but the passers-by just stop and frown.
Starving hungry and it's pouring down with rain
The day is almost over
I start to feel the pain
As I reach a little café and pull out my sack
Counting up my money as I go
I only have enough to buy me a roll
Off to find a dark place where I can sleep
A place of darkness a place of peace.

Stephanie Campbell (14)
Ursuline High School

Not My Business

I saw them take Isabelle this morning,
Shoved her round by the bins
I heard the pleas and cries
The contents of her bag hit the floor
But what have I got to do with it?
As long as I'm not the one left alone,
Trying to turn back time.

Damilola just vanished one day.
Was found bleeding to death
Smashed up with a bottle
And left to die in agony.
But what have I got to do with it,
As long as I'm not the one left alone,
Trying to turn back time.

They took Grace away one day
Took her grace away.
She was found lying in a puddle of blood
Gasping for breath in her few moments left
But what have I got to do with it
As long as I'm not the one left alone.
Trying to turn back time.

Poor Daniella was just shot one day
As the window rolled down
And the gun was revealed
There was nothing she could do.
But what have I got to do with it
As long as I'm not the one left alone.
Trying to turn back time.

Then one day as I turn the corner
There they are waiting for me,
Waiting, just waiting in their usual silence
And I can't go back they close in on me.
But now I have got something to do with it.
As I am just lying here alone.
Trying to turn back time.

Amy Luck (12)
Ursuline High School

Stone Cold

Stone cold lying on the floor,
People walking past and begging
They pay no attention, you feel like nothing,
You wish you had never left home.

Cry yourself to sleep every night
Hoping and wishing you were warm
People go, people come into your life
Each day, no money, no food.
You're not safe lying on that floor.

People come and steal from you,
Even the things most important to you.
But when you find a nice warm doorway
The police tell you to 'Push off.'

All around you see worn out faces,
In worn out places.
Suddenly you want to get up and look for a job,
But you can't, you just can't.

Your stone cold.

Jade Nartey
Ursuline High School

Days

Days are long,
No one's here.
Everyone's gone,
No one's here.
When I'm sleeping rough
No one's here.
When everything's tough,
No one's here.
No one's here I'm . . .
Invisible!

Rosalyn Duffy (13)
Ursuline High School

Living Rough

All day long I sit on the floor,
Begging for money, which I have no more.

I walk all night and I tap
But all I get is a big fat slap.

I have no reason to live my life,
I would really like a house and a wife.

I need a place to stay,
But people keep telling me to go away.

There's a killer about and I cannot shout,
My voice has gone and I really pong.

I'll say goodbye cause I'm gonna die,
He's gonna kill me, can't they see.

The police don't believe us,
They say we're making such a fuss,
I'm not gonna live, my life I will give.

Nathalie Moorghen (13)
Ursuline High School

A Poem On Sleeping Rough

Sleeping rough is horrible,
No clean clothes, food or water,
No warmth, friends or family around you,
Sleeping in a warm bed is much better.

At home there are rows,
But on the street there are rats,
You should be careful where you sleep,
Because you'll end up on someone's mat.

There are storms, thunder and lightning at night,
You'll never know who's round the corner,
Be careful where you are,
Because before you know it, you'll be a gonner.

Sophia Kyriacou (13)
Ursuline High School

A Lonely Man

I sit on the cold, hard floor
While people pass me, I'm seen no more.

I sit on the floor people chuck me money,
All I have enough for is a jar of honey.

This morning is wet and I'm on my own,
All I have left is a few skinny bones.

As I walk off and start to wonder
In my ear is a clap of thunder.

Sooner or later I will be history,
When I'm gone no one will miss me.

All my life I have never had a friend,
But soon it will be my life to an end.

Toya Islam-Sanchez
Ursuline High School

The Unsilent Night

The unsilent night was loud and fiery
Perhaps an event to record in your diary . . .

The willow tree wept as its branches broke.
The wind grew stronger, eerie with smoke
Thunder and lightning struck the sky
As an old owl was sleeping a bat started to fly.
When it too was hit by the thunder boom,
Lying dead on the ground full of sorrow and doom.

Thunder and lightning clapped their hands,
Black evil death tortured the lands,
Rain cackled roughly as it flooded the town
Little kids and parents in their sleep would all drown
Who is causing this vicious hell?
Is it the ringing of death's bell?
Is it nature weaving her spell?

Philippa Mann (12)
Ursuline High School

School Bullying

I went to school one morning,
Only to find you were ill,
I was all by myself that day,
Just standing there so still.

I sat down to do my work,
Oh how I tried so hard,
I couldn't concentrate,
I couldn't even make a card.

Without you there,
It wasn't much fun,
I could see them lurking behind me,
Where was the light from the sun?

They found me in the playground,
I tried hard not to scream,
But knowing me I couldn't resist,
So down I fell with a dream.

I woke up this morning,
Not in my cosy bed,
I was in a stranger's room,
'Where am I?' I said.

I arrived back home today,
My house was not the same,
It was full of loads of people.
Who came, came and came.

I go back to school tomorrow,
I know you'll be there to help me,
To guide me through the day,
So I won't be hiding, scared behind the tree.

Rebecca McGrath (12)
Ursuline High School

Not My Business

(Dedicated to Daniella and Damilola)

As they drove past in their car
Ready to shoot
Opened the tinted window
And *bang!*

What business of mine is it?
As long as they don't shoot me
I'll keep quiet.

Daniella was dead, left all alone
Why was she there?
Out late at night?
Parents suffering a lot - never to know
What really happened.

What business of mine is it?
As long as they don't shoot me
I'll keep quiet.

How fun was that computer lesson?
Walking home after school
Damilola really enjoyed his classes
Why did it have to go wrong?

What business of mine is it
As long as they don't stab me
I'll keep quiet.

Why was he there?
Lots of glass
Thigh injury
Left alone to die . . .

What business of mine is it?
As long as they don't stab me
I'll keep quiet.

Courtney Vincent (13)
Ursuline High School

A Ballad For Holly Wells And Jessica Chapman

We'll miss you here in Soham
Your lives have been so short
You trusted those who hurt you
The nation is distraught.

Your friends will weep for you
They stand alone and sad,
Your faces they will never forget
And all the good times you had.

David Beckham was your hero
His shirts walked side by side
On the day that you went missing
You both wore them with pride.

Your parents lost and lonely
They searched high and low
In every corner of Soham town
What happened and where did you go?

The people that have hurt you
May they feel the guilt,
They betrayed you
And the trust that you had built.

Your pictures on the television
And in the newspapers too,
Remind us of two little girls
We love but never knew.

May the angels guard you in Heaven
And for those you left behind,
Jessica and Holly, we'll never forget you
You'll always be in our minds.

Your friends will weep for you
They stand alone and sad,
Your faces they will never forget
And all the good times you had.

Ariana Remuiñan (13)
Ursuline High School

The End

Hooray! A human I see
But what is this?
He is trying to kill another human
Stop! I cry with no reply.

It seems that humans
Have killed each other
Not realising one thing
They are killing the human race.

I sit there crying
Everyone I knew gone
Oh I hate this place
And regret the wish.

I just want to go back home
To my family
This morning I said I hated them
But I'm really sorry.

I'm sorry my friend
For the other day
I had betrayed you
Or your secret rather.

If I were to know
That we were to come to this
I wouldn't have
Done anything in hatred.

Is that a gun
Aiming for me?
It won't hurt me really
As I am not really there.

Ouch! The pain
I thought it couldn't hit me
Make the pain stop
Oh, please make it stop.

Thick red fluid
Pouring out everywhere
And what is left of her
Is replaced on her bed.

Her mum comes in horror
Shocked at her death
For there was nothing to explain her death
But really it's only the beginning.

Arti Vaghela (11)
Ursuline High School

My World

My world is full of love and kindness
My world
My world
But this world is full of hatred and grief
This world
This world
I look back and see ugly faces
This world
This world
I look back and hear terrible whispers
This world
This world
I cannot hear or see any love
This world
This world
I will always go on knowing faraway is my world
My world
My world
Over and beneath will always be my world
My world
My world
In front and between will always be this world
This world
This world
Someday I will find my world
Someday
Someday.

Niamh Proctor (11)
Ursuline High School

Living In A Dream

I never want to wake
I'm living in this dream
It's better than reality
And nothing's what it seems.

Escaping my reality
Forgetting all my pain
Living in fake happiness
Willing to be sane.

People say I can't relate
And I don't even care
I try my best to understand
But it's more than I can bear

I hate the way that people
Always criticise me
Blinded by this ugliness
It's difficult to see.

I try my best to pass the test
It never goes my way
I want to do the best I can
But practise never pays

I know that if I scream
It won't take the pain away
I'm living in a dream
And that's where I want to stay.

Elvira Pandolfi (13)
Ursuline High School

Dreams

Can't somebody explain to me,
Why nothing's ever going to be,
Just the way you want it to seem,
But somehow it works out in your dreams.

You're all alone,
But you just can't breathe,
Everyone's saying you're to blame
And your heart's an anchor heavy with shame.

Nothing's ever like what it's going to be,
And eventually the pain turns into agony,
The wailing of your heart,
As it begins to slowly rip apart.

Everyone's at war with things,
Yet I'm at war with my heart,
In my dreams there are no wars,
Yet even there I'm still at war with my heart.

The pain is just too much to bear,
It's just as bad as the unknowing stare,
If you're misunderstood you're the one to blame,
Because no one else wants to share the shame.

Yet somehow it seems to hold together
In your dreams there's no stormy weather,
But in reality everything's falling apart,
At least in your dreams you're not a broken heart . . .

Tania Nadarajah
Ursuline High School

Every Time That I Complain

Every time I try to walk, I fall upon the ground
Every time I try to see, no sunlight can be found
Every time I try to hear, no one makes a sound
Nothing seems to work out right
This whole world's broken down.

Every time I see the sun, clouds form up ahead
Every time I try to smile, I seem to frown instead.
Every time I try to speak, there's nothing to be said.
Nothing seems to work out right
This whole world may be dead.

Every time I try to help, you turn and walk away
Every time I try my best, I'm ignored anyway
Every time my life gets bad, I close my eyes and pray
Nothing seems to work out right
This whole world thinks that way.

Caroline Draper (13)
Ursuline High School

My World

As I came down the steps
In front of me is a beautiful garden.
I can feel the light breeze against my face
The happy sound of children's laughter.
As I looked up the blue sky with birds singing
The smell of the fruity flowers brushing against my face.
In the distance I could see a gate I came closer to it,
I opened it then it suddenly turns dark.
I can hear the cooing of the owls my heart beating,
I'm scared then I see light that shines like the sun I stop in front of it.
I see it is a door
I can hear leaves rustling,
I go through the door and I am back in the classroom.

Elizabeth Lau (11)
Ursuline High School

The Storm

Lightning flashes
And thunder rolls
As the storm
Starts and grows.

Over the cliffs
And in the sea
Tosses and turns
Like sleepless me.

Banging windows
And swinging gate
Creak as they move
With the whistling wind.

The night grows darker
As the wind brings on
Pouring rain
One ordeal after another.

The lightning forks, flashing,
Really animate the startled sky
As the leaves from the trees
All fall
One
By
One.

After the storm
See the damage
A gate
In a tree
A tree
Fallen down
Several people dead I hear.

Despite the grandeur
The devastation that follows
Is like no other.

Helen Folkard-Baker (12)
Ursuline High School

Cloud Watcher

Have you noticed that clouds make shapes,
That only you can see?
The reason is you only see things
The way you think they should be.

Have you wondered why the world seems to turn on you all at once,
And nothing seems to go your way,
You don't know what you've done wrong,
But for some reason you have to pay,
Even when you try your best,
What ever you do is always just too late.

What has happened to the world today?
Everything's just one big mess,
Nothing seems to calm down
And good things just come less and less.
When all you want is to go back to the beginning
And start all over again
But then you realise there's no way of winning
The life long test.

Have you ever noticed it seems to rain,
When things start to go wrong,
And all you feel is pain.
The life you live
Just feels so wrong
But some how you find hope
And you keep holding on
Holding on to hope.

Rebecca Heath (13)
Ursuline High School

Weeping Woman Looking Sad

(Inspired by a photograph called 'Weeping Woman' by Picasso)

Weeping woman looking sad
People wonder why she isn't glad
Tears appear upon her face,
As people sigh a big disgrace.

Weeping woman looking sad,
People wonder why she isn't glad
She holds a tissue in her hand,
And listens to music by an Irish band.

Weeping woman looking sad
People wonder why she isn't glad.
She's dressed all in black,
And has her hair tied back.

Weeping woman looking sad
People wonder why she isn't glad
With eyes of blue
She wonders what she should do.

Weeping woman looking sad,
People wonder why she isn't glad,
She fears her husband's death,
And starts running out of breath.

Weeping woman looking sad,
People wonder why she isn't glad,
Her death comes in just a flash,
And her worries disappear in a dash.

Zubeida Osman (12)
Ursuline High School

Away

You took her away
Away for good
Nothing is she and she is nothing
Her soul gone up
Up to the heavens
Up to the stars, the moon and the sun
Sweet is what she whispers
I hear her call
You look away
Away for good

I run far
Far I run
Run past the heavens
Run past the stars, the moon and sun
Sweet I whisper to call her back
Hand in hand is how we walk
Together we fade away
And together and forever
We lay aside to rest.

Anne Attipoe
Ursuline High School

Wind

The warm wind flowing
The leaves of the tall oak tree blowing
My long black hair swaying.

The warm wind flowing
Plastic bags and food packets whizzing through the air,
Newspapers and important letters flying like birds.

The warm wind flowing
The leaves of the tall oak tree blowing
My long black hair swinging.

Kayeesha Gomes (12)
Ursuline High School

The Avalanche

Everything is calm,
Except a little breeze,
Along came heffers
And fell down on their knees.

The effect of this,
Made the snow begin to rumble,
Then some snow began to fall,
And the heffers fumbled.

Running hairy heffers,
Everywhere,
Same with the people,
They had not time to stop and stare.

'Avalanche' villagers screamed
Where should they go,
Falling, tumbling everywhere,
Was snow.

Not knowing what to do,
The villagers were squashed
By the herd of heffers,
That were covered in frost.

Snow as cold as ice,
As white as paper,
Where will it go?
Will it come back later?

The avalanche is over,
No more need to panic,
Everything is calm,
There's no manic.

Will there be another soon?
Will it come and see us?
I hope not, ever again!
I don't need anymore fuss.

Catherine Furlong (12)
Ursuline High School

Gold Is Me

I sit stirring cold coffee, waiting in Jo-Joe's café,
My loved one will be here soon I'm sure,
But when? That's the catch.

I've got the gold,
I've got the fur,
I've got the small pearl beads,
I've got the material and the money
After all, only this is me.

Jo-Joe stands chopping meat,
It's a tiring job -
There's a smile on his face,
It's not the money that matters with him -
It's his wife Mia, no material could replace.

I've got no love life,
I've got no friends,
I've got no company.
It really is hard,
I must keep strong,
After all only gold is me.

It's five years later, I have a new makeover,
I've got a brand new look,
It's now I know it's not the cover,
It's the information inside the book.

I'm trapped with no one to turn to,
No one to speak to,
Everything to say,
I guess that there's nobody in this world for me,
Material will have to stay my way.

Nancy Fagan (12)
Ursuline High School

1 Minute More

Can't you stay just 1 minute more?
Please don't leave me yet, please stay
There are so many things I haven't said
Like how beautiful you are, how funny you are
How much I love you, need you.

Don't embrace the darkness now
Don't leave me on my own
Stay in this world with me
Don't go into the cold.

Everyone says just 1 minute more
Never a second, an hour, a day, a week, a month, a year
A minute is long enough, but then never enough.
To say all that must be said, to do all that must be done.

So can't you stay just 1 minute more
Stay in this world with me.

Hannah Best (13)
Ursuline High School

Through The Gate

As I went through the gate, inside I felt a warm light breeze,
I smelt fresh air,
Towards me was a vast blue sea that shone in the sunlight,
And as the water came up towards me it tickled between my toes
As it cooled my feet down
Around me all was calm and peaceful nothing was disturbed
Far away in the distance I could hear some
                                    seagulls shouting a welcome at me.
A pathway ahead of me looked grand covered in flowers
                                    and new smells.
Unfortunately behind me I could feel someone tugging
                                    and calling me back
But I just couldn't leave I love it here!

Aimee Cunningham (12)
Ursuline High School

Ice Storm 1998

Electric pylons iced and gleaming
Crashed through my neighbours ceiling
Frozen truckers on the highway
Looking for a warm lay-by.

No electric, no gas, no heating
No way of cooking hot food for eating
Pensioners carried out of frozen flats
Wrapped in blankets carrying cats.

Trees bent double under the weight of ice
The TV is out and there's no hope of light
Listening to the radio hoping for good news
Will we get a hot shower today?
Will we get hot food?

I'm stuck in this motel with my mum and dad
My house is like an igloo, it's too bad
Has the world forgotten us all
The inhabitants of Montreal?

Lucy Rawlings (12)
Ursuline High School

Autumn Breeze

Autumn breeze whips through the air,
Reaching everyone, stopping nowhere,
Wrapping round your bones,
Pulling at your hair.
Autumn breeze is everywhere!

Rustling of the leaves, flying in the air,
Round and round in circles, like they don't care!
They'll swoop down to your ankles.
Or get stuck in your hair,
Autumn breeze is everywhere!

Now it's time to settle down, autumn's drifting away,
Everybody wraps up warm, winter's here to stay!

Dannielle Leonard (12)
Ursuline High School

Desert Island

Dear Captain,
I don't know why I am here,
I can't believe you threw me overboard with just a bottle of beer.

I know I was a pain and was so lazy
But I think what you did is being a bit crazy.

Remember the time I helped you find all that gold,
With only rags of clothes you gave me you dumped me in the cold.

Since I have been in this place for *three days,*
I now know how to understand the island's ways.

Don't be up late, not enough food because of other living things
But beside there's something that wakes me up early morning, it rings

Captain, I can describe to you what the island looks like,
It's dull, and colourless I like to see the mountains just to take a hike.

Dear Captain will be stuck here for another two years,
Me all alone with just my thoughts and fears.

Dear Captain,
Funny how this is not real,
The prison is the desert island, garbage they serve as a meal.

The ringing to signal the early start of the day,
To me a signal, an attempt to get a morsel of food (out of my way).

Prison, I hate it here I can't believe you told them that I did a crime,
A crime I didn't commit, because of you I'm in a place full of crime.

Two years I come out,
Captain when I get out always be in doubt.

Charlotte Napoleon-Kuofie (12)
Ursuline High School

The Almighty Gale

The gale was fearsome
Crushing the windows with its fists.
It had come to destroy all that lay in its way.
Howling and shouting that all shall obey
Terrifying fragile plants into tiny little pieces.

The one time a weatherman gets it perfectly right
There's a gale trying to destroy my house
I decided I was going to put up a fight, I had the right.

I shut the windows locked the doors,
Turned up the heating,
And covered up the chimneys with building boards.

The noise was horrendous
The smell was horrendous
The feeling was horrendous.

Suddenly the dawn came,
The gale had gone and all was quiet.

Helen Tanner **(12)**
Ursuline High School

Our House

Our house in the middle of our street
Our house is never ever neat
Our house is a pickle and a mess
Our house is noisy but the best.

Our house 4 girls and 3 boys
Our house is always full of noise
Our house the food is always great
Our house you'll always have a mate.

Our house 12 rooms and 3 floors
Our house we always need more space
Our house
Our house.

Lucy McDonald **(13)**
Ursuline High School

Serenity

As I gripped the icy gate,
I felt a cold feeling throughout my hand.
I pushed the gate open and I had a great feeling
                    of calm and peacefulness
As I walked through the garden my feet touched
                    the warm and gentle grassy path below.
The great scents of roses and lavender sent
                    a waft of serenity through me.
Nothing else was on my mind apart from the gracious garden.
Across the garden was an enormous mango tree
                    full of lovely ripe juicy mangos.
I reached out and peeled back the smooth textured skin
                                        and took a bite.
I felt the sweet juice trickle down my chin;
It was the most satisfying taste I had ever experienced.
Next to the tree was a fountain of water trickling down the rocks,
                                        the sound was so peaceful.
I laid down taking in the sounds and the scents.
It was so tranquil I wanted to hold on to that moment forever.

Katie Kemp (11)
Ursuline High School

Freedom

(Inspired by 'A Dream Landscape')

I seem to be torn between two,
The ocean and the sky blue,
There are huge metal bars blocking my way,
Blocking me from the cool ocean spray.
My other choice an open field,
Where the trees are my shield.
Which one I will choose,
I don't know,
I think to the ocean's flow.
My reason to choose this,
Well it's home to my food the fish.

Natasha D'souza (12)
Ursuline High School

Earthquakes

'It's here'
It has a hatred for us
As strong as a twister
'It has no trust'

'It's here'
Making us all fall to our knees
To beg for forgiveness
For awakening them.

It's here
Waiting for me
To come and see
Just how much it hates me.

'It's here'
And suffering its lust!
Its need of pain
And has a craving for sadness
You see that's why it wants me.

'It's here'
Left me
To fight all alone
I've won the battle
'But I'm on my own'.

'It's gone'
No more pain
But survived my new mission
'Tomorrow the only vision I see.'

'It's gone'
In ruins
It left my home
Bodies scattered beaten and bruised
'Still is the atmosphere.'

'It's gone'
So I can build up my home again
To bring back life
'To live life as best I can'

'You see it was here and now it's gone!'

Massah Tucker (12)
Ursuline High School

Not My Business

Powerful punch, swing left to right,
Silence fell,
Bruises formed,
Blood wet, skin torn,
Helplessly I stood in the darkened distance
No business of mine
Oh well! The world goes on . . .

Powerful kick, swing left to right,
Happiness a thing of the past,
Held like a prisoner,
Forever the prey.
Helplessly, I stood in the darkened distance
No business of mine
Oh well! The world goes on . . .

Powerful slap, swung left to right
The smile on his face left astray,
Harshly tamed,
Never to react,
Left attacked
Helpless I stood,
Upon the boy
Suddenly my heart stopped with guilt . . .

Brooklyn Kerlin (12)
Ursuline High School

I Have A Dream

I have a dream
Where the skies of blue gleam
Where freedom and peace roam
Where no one is alone.

I have a dream
Where happiness will last
War, a forgotten past
Where evil can never be cast.

I have a dream
Where friendship is forever
Friends stick like glue together
Like birds of a feather.

I have a dream
Where hunger and famine is not
Something lived through and forgot
In our memories the size of a dot.

I have a dream
Where prejudice has been left to lie
Discrimination has faded and died
And no one is cunning or sly.

I have a dream
A dream of a worry free world
For every adult, every girl, every boy,
Never is forced to feel saddened or coy.

I have a dream
Where in every town, every city and street
Where people welcome, appreciate, greet
No matter the person they meet.

I dare to have a dream
A dream unlike no other
A dream of the prefect world.

Angela Musoke
Ursuline High School

Darkness

I do my teeth then rest my head,
Upon the pillow on my bed,
I pull the cover over me,
And switch the light off cosily,
Darkness starts to fill the room
Every word I read is doom,
Then nightly sky has turned dark black,
The pavement has its ghostly crack,
The streets are quiet no one here,
Darkness fills my eyes with fear,
I need someone here to talk,
I cannot go for a simple walk,
I'm scared to death as you can see,
Darkness is taking over me,
Don't let it get me, keep me safe,
All I need's a little faith,
If I can sleep through just one night,
Then maybe things will be all right.

Laura Planson (12)
Ursuline High School

Blink And You'll Miss It

Years go by, like seconds past
Childhood memories are the ones that last.

Like endlessly drifting in an ocean of time,
Like reading an essay all in mime.

You'll grow and change, then change again
You'll move away and make new friends.

From child to adult in a minute flat,
Blink and you'll miss it,
It's as quick as that.

Freddie Joynt (14)
Ursuline High School

Snowstorm

The wind brushed past my roughened face
At a swift, humid, speedy, rushed pace.
A snowdrop flickered in my eye,
Made it water then I cried.

The snow was falling in heaps and boulders
Most of the snow was piled up on my shoulders?
As I walked through the downpour of snow,
It him my face and I went pale.
Then along came a gale force blow.

The snow was tender, soft and white,
I knew that by the time I'd got home I'd have frostbite!
My arms were in agony from my heavy sack,
I nearly fell to the floor and broke my back.

I'm almost out now, of the storm,
I'll never go through it again if I'm normal?

Lady Coleman (12)
Ursuline High School

Hurricane

Rapidly twisting, winding, storming in the blink of an eye.
Cows flying, cattle dying, cars demolished,
People fleeing, trees dropping - non stopping.
Houses damaged, lives ruined, lives taken.
The grim reaper soaring by.
Do you dare look it in the eye?
You can run, but you can't hide
It will come, when
It's your time. So
I warn you with
This rhyme.
It is deadly
It's insane,
It is a -
Hurricane.

Lani Manuel (13)
Ursuline High School

There Is An Ice Age Going On

The whole of Europe is white,
No one knows what to do,
There are giant balls of ice falling from the sky;
There is an ice age going on.

Hundreds, thousands, millions of people are gone,
Families are destroyed; the world will never be the same again,
Bodies are scattered on the ground, like marbles to a floor;
There is an ice age going on.

Confused, mixed up faces,
Scare and fear is around
Death is the foulest smell,
There is an ice age going on.

Isolation, emptiness and stillness,
The world has been destructed,
Why has this happened to us, *why, why, why;*
An ice age has just gone on.

Rachel D'Souza (12)
Ursuline High School

The Flood

T he flood was tragic
H ow could it destroy everything
E veryone was astonished, it created so much disaster.

F ailing to stop, failing to care
L arge waves kept crashing over and over again
O nly a fool wouldn't run
O nly a genius would
D amaging, wrecking, running, bashing, spoiling everything.

Emily Figueira (12)
Ursuline High School

Alone

The sun is blazing down upon my weak back,
Ahead I see a tap with refreshing water flowing out,
Alas it was just a mirage.
My feet are burning with the heat of the sand,
I can barely walk a step further
I walk steadily up a sandy cliff and spot fresh green grass.
Water, something living and healthy
I race forwards falling over my feet
My eyes must be playing tricks on me.
Somebody is sitting in a shaded area drinking from a flask and talking
to someone on a phone
I observe who the person is and recognise the someone suddenly
It's our tour guide calling a rescue patrol
I race towards him my face glowing
We talk together about how we got left behind,
Around 15 minutes later we are in safe hands and on our way home.

Amy Clarke (11)
Ursuline High School

Untitled

A friend is like a tree
All their different personalities
Are the branches
The ways they show them are the leaves.

A good friend is someone you carry through life,
When you fall they catch you,
When you cry they comfort you,
When you are happy they rejoice with you.

Sometimes there are friends that don't stick around,
But a true friend will stay by your side.

Do you catch?
Do you comfort?
Do you rejoice?
Are you a true friend?

Grace Corriette
Ursuline High School

Get Me Off This Rock!

It's only been two weeks,
It feels like an eternity.
Being stranded on this island,
Makes me feel like Carrie, and me
Are the only two people on the Earth.

It's strange how such a beautiful and inviting place,
Can be so lonely, depressing and empty.
Carrie tries her best to be positive.
But supplies are running low,
And only one boat has gone by . . .

That was our saddest day yet,
We really thought they were going to save us,
We really thought we were going home.
Carrie's voice was hoarse from yelling
All I could do was wave my arms and shout,
'Get me off this rock!' As we watched
It sail into the horizon and slowly disappear.

Alana O'Sullivan (11)
Ursuline High School

You Look At Me And Forget

There she stands alone on the sidewalk.
Lonely and forgotten - no one to care.
No one to share her pain with,
She feels discriminated and hated, that she is not loved.
Tears roll down her cheeks desperate to be included.
There she stands outcast, excluded and forgotten.

Antonia Ayodele
Ursuline High School

God

All my life I have wondered about God,
How big and tall He is,
Or what He looks like.
I have come to realise that He is Great.
I definitely know that He is not a mistake.
Without Him, where would we be?
What would we do?
And who are we?
God is our comforter and cheers us up when we are sad
He's there to support us, even when times are bad.
Even though we do not notice that He is here,
We should be bold, strong and never fear.
For God is listening to our prayers with an opened ear.
We should be more appreciative and thankful of Him,
Because if it wasn't for Him, we would be people living in sin.
And when it comes to judgement day,
I will shout aloud, declare and say.
God is my everything and I love Him dearly,
And that I am ready to join Him in Heaven and to see more clearly.

Isabella Amfo (13)
Ursuline High School

Snow

In the air white snowflakes fall
Some are big, some are small.

On the ground they gather together
I wish this snow would last forever.

Everyone is playing with snowballs too.
It's good until they land on you.

Harley-Mae Brennan
Ursuline High School

Hurricane

The sky darkens and its grimace begins to show.
The wind whistles like a choir,
The sky chuckles like a clown,
But as for the noise it slays the whole town.

The children bellow for their parents,
The parents shriek for their children,
Stuck and injured people try to phone for help
As the phone lines blaze uncontrollably
Poor animals lay there feeble mindedly.

Houses cry for their bricks to stay in line
Poor, short and furious people yelp for shelter
Members of churches bow down to pray,
This is a bloodcurdling, awfully, horrible day.

It separates friends,
It separates loved ones,
It separates love and everything else.

You see your belongings scrunch one by one,
You wonder where the end is going to be,
But you can't see.
This is the horrible abominable, atrocious day.

Vanessa Acquah (12)
Ursuline High School

Untitled

I came down the stairs,
And there in front of me was a colourful land.
I took my shoes off, beneath my feet
Where the prickly tips of the grass and leaves
The breeze was as cold as the winter snows,
The sun was as yellow as gold.

Next to me were bushes
Full of strawberries.
There at the end of the lane
Was a little gate so far away.

I walked down towards the gate
And as I went through, a strong smell came towards me,
I crept near it,
Keeping as quiet as a mouse,
In front of me was a family,
Sitting around the table.

They asked me to join and I said OK
Then we go out and play
Through the rustling of the trees
Is a faint sound of water trickling down.

Megan Evans (11)
Ursuline High School

Beautiful Cold Winter

B ye bye summer, hello winter
E arth is changing
A ll around us is cold especially in winter
U sing our hats, scarves, coats and gloves.
T ime going on and on like the season is never going to end
I t will soon be Christmas before you know it
F ive little snowflakes touching your hand then more and more
U mbrellas are up before the snow can touch you
L ightly, lightly ever so lightly the snow floats down to the ground.

C old and shivering
O n your doorstep wait to get in your lovely house
L ovely and warm at last in your house
D rinking hot cocoa tucked up in a blanket.

W inter is here all so soon
I cicles everywhere from the rain
N ear is Christmas cold and white
T ops of roofs covered in snow
E verywhere is white including your clothes
R ather hoping that summer will come soon.

Louisa Akwaboah (11)
Ursuline High School

All Alone . . .

All alone on a piece of land,
Wondering where I am,
Not knowing if there's any life.
Everywhere you look is water
Just pure blue water!

A step at a time
In the hot burning sand
Because of the fiery sun
It burns all day.
While I try to find shade!

It's getting darker
I'm scared to my depths,
Of the strange sounds at night.
Whatever will jump out on me
I have not a clue?

Maybe tomorrow will be better.
Again the sun will shine
I will be able to see the blue water
And maybe someone will find me,
Save me from this dry area!

Saaleha Idrees (12)
Ursuline High School

Untitled

I walked through a brown wooden gate to feel . . .
Beneath my feet I felt the long ticklish grass
In front of me I could see,
The old brown green-leafed tree.

Down the rough concrete path I went just to see . . .
Around the trees that I could see
Were bunches of yellow roses for me.

Behind the trees I could see a small
Cottage, which faced directly at me.

Through the ticklish grass I walked
Towards the cottage to see . . .
A group of humming birds.
Humming on an old magic tree.

Next to me I could see an
Old, rusty, gold key
I bent down to pick it up
But my mum called me back for tea.

I ran down the path
Across the green ticklish grass
Through the gate back to my house.

Sian Varney (12)
Ursuline High School

Life Of The Homeless

Some people have money
Some people have none
Some people are rich -
Live in a world of comfort and greed
Some people have no money at all
Not even enough to feed.
Sometimes it's not their fault
They don't know why they live in the subs.
But some people spend their money
On cigarettes and drugs
And no matter how they got that way,
I pity them and their lives
When I sit at home in front of the fire,
I wonder 'how would I survive?'
The people of London do nothing
Because you can't trust a stranger.
Why? Because they are dirty.
But you're not always right.
Sometimes the stranger does love the neighbour
Though you'll never know
And still homeless people have nowhere to go.

Florence Cleverdon (13)
Ursuline High School

The Shipwreck

Whilst trudging through golden sand
The snakes and lizards own the land,
And the boiling sun burns my neck,
I walk away from the sunken shipwreck.

I wander through scared and alone
While in the trees, the monkeys moan
Then suddenly a silence rips through my ears,
As I discover my worst fears.

Day turns to night and I feel so alone
And through the forest I roam and roam
While the sun sets over the gleaming ocean
Everything seemed to be in slow motion.

The dazzling moon shines through the trees
And all around me mosquitoes and bees
The buzzing and hovering annoyed me so much
But after a while it didn't annoy me as such.

I woke up confused and scared
But something caught my eye and I glared and glared.
A ship on the horizon, do my eyes deceive me?
But I thought to myself from this island, I am free!

Heather Clayton (11)
Ursuline High School

All Alone . . .

I sat, watching the stars in the sky,
Listening to all the owls cry,
Nothing to eat, nothing to do,
All I can see is this blur of blue
I realised I am crying again,
My heart is broken, filled with pain.

Drenched with rain, my shelter is a tree,
Nothing to hear, nothing for me,
The cotton ball clouds that used to be white,
Had changed to grey over the nights
This small little island, all alone
I wish, I wish I could be at home.

Stranded, abandoned, empty, lost, nothing inside,
20 days 20 nights, still there is nothing to find,
It just feels like I've disappeared,
My brain is nothing completely cleared
I don't know am I dead or alive?
Or maybe I will be on TV, to tell the world I survived.

Aimee Newell (11)
Ursuline High School

Blizzard

It starts off with a chilly breeze
Small snowflakes drip from the sky
Then the puddles start to freeze,
The birds suddenly cease to fly.

A small clump of lonely houses,
Surrounded by icy fields.
A cloud then slowly closes,
Emptiness, loneliness, lost, silence.

Then the snow starts to fall,
Then the wind starts to blow,
Then the mothers start to call,
Then the river stops flowing.

It chases after everyone,
Like a dangerous beast,
You know when it has begun,
Coldness, helplessness, fright, danger.

Out of the window all you see
Is icy white with a streak of blue
A blanket of white not a patch of green,
All the snowflakes sticking like you
I know, so do you
A blizzard has started.

Camille Auclair (13)
Ursuline High School

Alone

The sun is beaming down on me,
Swept here to this place,
I cannot face the awful sea,
Another day I face.

Suddenly I had to go,
I felt I had been seen,
Then again how can I know?
What it is I mean.

Alone throughout the endless day,
I gather wood for the fire,
I see a ship in the distance and pray,
To be rescued is my desire.

The ship is coming near,
I wait for it to see me,
For it to leave me is my fear,
But finally there with me.

I'm eventually on my way home,
Safe and sound at last,
No more need to be alone,
Across the water I go.

Now I'm not alone!

Tessa Whistler
Ursuline High School

Icy Touch

In Lapland a white crisp day
Nothing has come out to play,
No warmth no sound
Just still and silent
All around.

But all at midnight
It would change
For the icy touch
Was on its way . . .

The only life or colour in this place,
Are the still fir trees and small lakes,
He will creep through,
And make everything glow white,
Like everything else in sight
To a gentle snowdrop
To a strong oak tree.

The sky flew slowly over
As if a big black duvet
Black as a panther with a large grey smile
That shimmers and glistens,
The icy touch had come,
Then came the sun that shone over the land
That was white and bland, silent and still.
The icy touch has frozen the land and always will.

Hayley-May Smith (12)
Ursuline High School

My Desert Life

This place is so empty that even my soul has
Become a vacant space
And now I am hounded by the intense night
This devil of a night
The implication of this night -
I may die.

Taken by the cold
Or in daylight
Harassed by the burning light
With parchment skin
Moistureful me eradicated.

A sandstorm starts
I'm eating sand burdened wind
A thousand needles pierce my eyes
My body is trammelled
I am drowning in this sea of sand.

I am stranded here
My home has left me
And the desert leaves me ensnared.

With no one to know me I have lost my name
I am nobody
As this body confronts
Extreme weather
Succumbing to its grip.

Domenica George (11)
Ursuline High School

Silence Of The Lambs

Co-dependent, no more am I,
Beyond co-dependency, I am,
I've observed the way, that things are,
And identified the way things should be,
In order to find a deeper meaning of reality.

As meaningless as I am, as meaningless as the sea,
You can't take away my being,
Even if you don't acknowledge me.
Psychologically, I'm affected,
But I have a legacy.
And I refuse to be affected,
By your negativity.

So if rules are there to be broken,
Then I'll take my chance and rule break,
Because I know the way things should be,
Yet I refuse to partake,
In a system,
Which denies me,
The finding of my voice,
But acknowledge that,
Words will turn to actions
When I am given the choice.

As shameless as my life is to you,
As shameless as I am,
I don't care what decision you have come to
This is not the silence and I am not a lamb.

Latisha Royer (16)
Ursuline High School

The Desert's Next Victim

I open my eyes and look around me,
There's nothing to hear there's little to see,
There's sand to the left there's sand to the right
It's pitch-black dark in the middle of the night.

As the horizon breaks with warm sunlight,
I shield my eyes the rays are so bright,
I feel the warmth creeping up my back,
As I stagger along the long sand track.

The heat continues to pound down in this hot land,
There's no water here it's nothing but sand,
The heat overcomes me I can't carry on,
The path that lies ahead seems too long.

I drop on the ground I'm too tired to stand,
I close my eyes as I lie in the sand,
The sun is above me the heat is so strong,
I can't stand it anymore the day is so long.

As the sun stays high as the day draws on
I knew I'd have to find shade before long,
Finally the cool night came again,
I had to be rescued but the question was when.

I was really hungry, I was really thirsty,
But still no water as far as I could see,
I can't last any longer I have to rest,
I can't survive out here but I tried my best.

Catriona Thompson (11)
Ursuline High School

Alone

The snow falls down,
To the iced up ground
I've been here for days,
But haven't been found.

I want to snuggle up
In my warm cosy bed,
I wish I wasn't here
But at home instead.

Eating fish
Isn't very nice
I want to go home
To eat chicken and rice!

If only my plane hadn't crashed
I wouldn't be here shivering
My whole body feels numb
I am always quivering.

I want to get out of here
I want to go home now
When am I ever going to be rescued?
When, and how . . .?

Lauren Rann (11)
Ursuline High School

Disaster Holiday

As the sunrays came down beating on our necks,
I wish I had some water nice and cool.
I remembered the scene as the plane came down crashing,
Everything was black.

I heard some voices
I remembered I was with my family and friends
I was not alone,
The sun started to come down,
It was getting darker.

We all knew that we had to make a shelter,
Find food and water also,
We all started to look around the island,
The sand was burning my feet.
We got some palm leaves and wood.

I looked for some bananas or coconuts,
Nice juicy fruits,
But nothing.
Then at the corner of my eye I saw something,
A coconut and another then lots more
I had some faith put in my heart.

Katherine Navarro (11)
Ursuline High School

A Dry Wasteland

The blazing sun beat down on me,
And my crashed helicopter.
I had a bad head injury, but I had a first aid kit,
So I was lucky to be alive.

I couldn't find food,
I couldn't find water,
But I found wood for shelter.

The nights were as cold as ice,
But the days were hot,
Boiling hot
Hotter than the hottest volcano.

Wherever I looked
Wherever I turned,
All I could see was cliffs.
Big cliffs, small cliffs, daringly dangerous cliffs.
The kind of cliffs that can kill you.

The gorges were long and cold
Very high, very bold
The feel of an everlasting doom,
Rushed around my head like wild fire, as if the heat wasn't bad
enough.

I had heat frustration and dizziness
I fall to my hands and knees,
Then I saw something,
A rescue team
Coming to take me away
Away from that dry, desert wasteland.

Charlotte Murtagh (11)
Ursuline High School

As I Stare Into Space . . .

As I stare into space I see,
A beautiful world surrounding me,
Peace and happiness all around,
Everything is safe and sound,
But the world isn't like this,
It is covered with war and death.

As I stare into space I see,
Everything I want to see,
Love and kindness, generosity,
A world filled with tranquillity,
But the world isn't like this,
It is surrounded with war and death.

As I stare into space I see,
Happiness all around me,
Everyone is sweet and kind,
There is no sadness, I think you'll find
But the world isn't like this
It is filled with war and death.

As I listen I can hear,
All that I want to hear,
Silence, silence,
If we all stick together,
Be kind and generous to each other,
Then the world will be like this,
It won't be filled with war and death anymore.

Chloe Proctor (12)
Ursuline High School

Why Can't I Be Normal?

Why can't I be normal?
Why is it when all the children come?
They stop, and start to point at me,
And then they go and run.

Why can't I be normal?
I just stay awake at night
Waiting for the day to come,
Waiting for the fright.

Why can't I be normal?
Why did it all have to begin
Whenever I look at my father,
He looks at me like I'm nothing.

Why can't I be normal?
Why does my dad have to hit me
He tells me he didn't mean it,
But when I look in his eyes I can see.

Why can't I be normal?
I'm going to run away.
I just can't go on living like this
I just can't bear to stay.

Alex Tanner (12)
Ursuline High School

The Hurricane

Drifting and swirling, up and down,
Twisting and turning all around.
It starts off small then humongously bigger
The sound is like a massive digger.

It collects things while on its way,
Dragging things away and away.
It makes unhappy noises through the square
It can also leave people in great despair.

Unhappiness is what's inside people's mind.
While the hurricane disposes rubbish behind.
The place is like havoc now,
Yet I am still not quite sure how.

It can be a real nightmare for some
As we crowd together and hug each other as one,
It was a really tragic and awful day,
And everyone didn't know quite what to say.

Now it's gone, not to come back again,
As it has caused so much stress and pain
It's all back to normal now
But still people are wondering how.

Amani Radeef (12)
Ursuline High School

Volcano

Normal place, normal time, normal silence
Everything still, everything quiet, everything calm.
But then . . .
Whoosh!
The volcano erupts!
The quiet village is interrupted of its normal silence
It's hot, dry and hard to breathe,
The inhabitants run to shelter as fire streams across the land.

Adults run, children cry, it's hard, it smells of burning
Everyone is terrified and everyone is anxious
Scientists say but how can it be
This volcano hasn't erupted since 1683!
I suppose it will always be a mystery.

People are recovering, but everyone is sticking together
But then one, just one decides I'll go my own way
I do not want this . . . he goes.

So this one man decides to live elsewhere
But then, oh no! Another volcano erupts there!
He has learnt his lesson, he must go back
Normal place, normal silence, normal time.

Maria Garcia (12)
Ursuline High School

No Way!

They picked on Danny the other day,
I saw him he started to pray!
People took the mick out of him, as he went to church
I didn't help, if I did they'd take my brand new walkman
No way!

During maths, Susy was chosen,
She was the paper bin!
I thought, should I say something?
I didn't help; if I did they'd take my brand new walkman
No way!

Cameron was the next target for the vultures
They followed him to a pace, and then it started to look like a race
They punched and punched 'til a puddle of red came!
I didn't help; if I did they'd take my brand new walkman
No way!

The vultures were picking on some girl today
I was speechless, I didn't know what to say!
The girl was *me!*
I squealed and squealed they took my walkman
I said no way, they said yes today!
I shouted and shouted, 'no way!'

Jordan Butler (12)
Ursuline High School

Who Will Come For Me?
(From Chinese Cinderella)

I was born - what for?
Has anyone noticed I'm alive?
Who cares? But I'm waiting here . . .
Who will come for me?

Never loved or heard,
Never offered or privileged,
Always bullied and left out,
I'm in a dark and deep tunnel,
Though I'm still waiting here . . .
Who will come for me?

All alone, no one to talk to,
No one to share my dreams with
Lying on my bed, looking at nothing,
Thinking of nothing,
But I've waited here . . .
Nobody has come for me.

My life was like a horror scope,
I was unhappy, and in mourning,
I didn't know who I was,
But I've waited here . . .
Somebody has come for me.

Venessa Vas (13)
Ursuline High School

Volcanoes

Volcanoes are two-faced
One side's peaceful,
The other is a living hell.
When it's angry it thinks hate.
It lets out an almighty roar
Then it overturns and all the hate comes crawling out.

It spreads across the land,
Everything that was once good goes bad.
People screaming, all petrified.
All because one things anger!
Houses fall down and people dying.
It's sad.

When it is happy with what it's done
It stops all the bad
And all is peaceful again
But no birds singing,
No animals eating,
No people laughing,
No children playing.

Hate and anger kill
So does volcanoes!

Sasha Thompson (12)
Ursuline High School

Open Desert

Standing here in this desert wasteland alone,
The fiery sun beating down,
My head thinking round and round,
How did I get this way?
That's all I can say.

Soft sand in my lunch
So when I bite it makes a crunch
How did it get this way?
That's all I can say.

No one knows I am here,
We should have gone to Cerea,
How did we get this way?
That's all I can say.

Walking on and on
Fighting 'till the battle is won,
How did I get this way?
That's all I can say.

It's night-time now,
And I'm scared and thirsty,
Having thoughts about my family and best friend,
Will this starvation ever end?
How did life get this way?
That's all I can say.

Rachel Childs (11)
Ursuline High School

Stranded

The sky can look beautiful
But not when you're lying stranded,
In the empty desert,
With the cursed fireball's rays glaring down at you,
I was so weak I couldn't even get up
I felt my hope disintegrating,
My luck drowned.

Lost in my thoughts, I think about how I got there,
I received flashbacks of falling through the clear blue sky,
And how I landed 'plonk' on my bum,
It was funny to me, I just managed to smile a bit,
My head suddenly started spinning
And my body shook violently, the heat had triggered my epilepsy,
I lay there in pain; I could only wait for it to pass.

Pictures of my family went through my head like a slide show,
Slowly I realised that there was no point in trying to survive,
With no water or food there wasn't anything to keep me alive
I closed my eyes and lay in the sun.

Just as I was ready to die I was woken by a continuous beep
When I woke up in hospital very confused
My family watched over me certainly not amused
Everyone thought I had died
They were all wrong I survived
Thank the Lord in the sky.

Anne Pushpanathan
Ursuline High School

Stranded

There I was sitting watching the waves go in and out,
Watching what was happening around and about,
My friend was in the background finding things to help our wounds,
I could hear in my ear all these magical tunes,
She bought over two coconut milks and I lay back to rest my head,
All I was thinking of was my family at home and my nice warm bed.
As the night fell upon us the stars in the sky appeared,
I made a fire to keep all animals clear,
Then out of the sun began to shine, or this little island
my friend and me were on,
As the fiery hot sun beat down on us it was hard to find shade,
Every bit of my body was in pain,
It was better than in old school by getting hit with the cane.
I dreamt of back home with my family and friends
Wishing I could be with them
Will we ever get out of here 'cause I'm close to dying
I am sick and tired of trying
My eyes were glassed over with tears of fright
There was no one there no one in sight,
A saw a ship sailing towards us
We were jumping up and down in such a fuss,
Then we were going home and we will never be alone
We get rescued and sail away,
Leaving that island alone to that day.
Now I'm at home all snuggled up tight,
I'm always ready for the deep, deep night!

Kerry Moriarty
Ursuline High School

2 Doves And An Apple Tree

It was a chilled spiritless Christmas
The wind was howling
As the purified white snow tumbled to the ground.

The snow was white
As pure as an angel
But not the snow covered nation.

The sweet smell of pinewoods and succulent cranberries
Wasn't even enough to cover up the terror
That had over come the country over the last few months.

As the beautiful doves flew into the magnificent apple trees
The dove fell to the floor as the trees collapsed
And the apples fell to their grave.

The world was stunned
For these apples they were
The traders of the world and the trees they were protectors
Though that's done and dusted.

As I look into a small little house,
I see a small little family
Surrounding a magnificent, glistening green Christmas Tree.

They're happy as happy as can be
The once spiritless Christmas
Now has a cool bliss of happiness that will last forever.

Earleatha Oppon (12)
Ursuline High School

His Eyes Have Seen All

(Inspired by the film 'Korczak' and by a story that my grandfather told me about the Holocaust)

His eyes have seen all
He'd tried to warn them,
Ovens, showers, hair and shoes
His eyes have seen all.

He'd seen them all fall,
People, children, grandmothers,
Grandfathers, trains and suitcases
His eyes have seen all.

He'd heard all the calls
'Edek!' 'Tomek!' 'Anna!' 'Esther!'
'Mother!' 'Father!' 'Aunt!' 'Uncle!'
His eyes have seen all.

He knew all the words,
Heil, hail, rain, wind, blue
Blonde, white, snow, go. No!
His eyes have seen all.

The pleas he has heard
'I'm American!' 'I'm catholic!'
'I'm blonde!' 'I'm rich!'
His eyes have seen all.

He'd not heard the shout
'Stand to attention, get up
Stand up, oh God . . . '
His eyes see nothing.

Sofi Izbudak (12)
Ursuline High School

You Look At Me

When I get home
You look at me
Like I'm someone else
I wish one day I would come home
To a smiling face that welcomes me inside
With strong arms to hold me tight
When I start to cry and there's no point
In going on
Wishing for such a thing is a myth
I only want love
But that boat is sailing further and further away
The scars on my back will fade
But the memories I've locked away
Will always stay and haunt me in my dreams
You look at me and I remember all the
Time I spent in fear wondering when the pain will end.

I love my school I always will
Nothing can change my mind
It's the only place I can escape
From the murderess look in her eyes
As I grew up I learned a lot and when my father died
They say it all went to her
When Niang had passed away we found a piece of paper
On it was my father's will
He loved me and that was all I ever wanted
I know now that dreams and wishes can come true.

Louise Carter (12)
Ursuline High School

Not My Business

They mugged him,
Hurt him beat him up
Stole the phone from his baggy pants
What business is it of mine?
So long as they don't take my new Nokia phone.

They snuck up on her,
From behind her unaware back,
And grabbed her phone as she was chatting back.
What business is it of mine?
So long as they don't take my new Nokia phone.

Lightoin was running home one day
And stopped to count her cash from today.
They ran up behind her and snatched her purse laughing.
What business is it of mine?
So long as my purse is in my bag.

And then one night,
On my way strolling home,
They came up behind me and stole my phone as I was chatting back,
And my purse as I was counting my cash.
Hey, I shouted as they ran away,
Laughing, but what business is it of theirs,
Their phones are in their bags.

Elizabeth Nyenwe (13)
Ursuline High School